THE COMMANDO

THE LIFE AND DEATH OF
Cameron Baird, VC, MG

BEN MCKELVEY

WITH THANKS TO KAYE AND DOUG BAIRD

hachette
AUSTRALIA

Soldiers in the SASR and 2 Commando have protected identity status, and therefore the names of currently serving members have been changed. The names of deceased and retired operators have not been changed.

A Note about the Taliban
It's likely that many of the anti-government forces that Cameron Baird confronted in Afghanistan were not under direct Taliban control. Sometimes fighters were the militia of a local warlord or drug kingpin, or part of a tribal group aligned with the Taliban. Sometimes they were not aligned with the previous actors but had some motivation to resist. It's difficult to properly catalogue many of the enemy combatants in the chapters to come, so, in the interests of simplicity, and so as to be aligned with most other reporting, any combatant who raised a gun against coalition troops in the Afghanistan conflict will usually be referred to as a 'Taliban'.

'THE MILE' (words and music by Kim Benzie/Robert Maric/Scott Davey/Stewart Hill/Forrester Savell) © Universal Music Publishing Pty Ltd. All rights reserved. International copyright secured. Reprinted with permission.

hachette
AUSTRALIA

First published in Australia and New Zealand in 2017
by Hachette Australia
(an imprint of Hachette Australia Pty Limited)
Level 17, 207 Kent Street, Sydney NSW 2000
www.hachette.com.au

This edition published in 2018

10 9 8 7 6 5 4 3 2 1

NATIONAL LIBRARY OF AUSTRALIA

A catalogue record for this book is available from the National Library of Australia

ISBN: 978 0 7336 4080 3 (paperback)

Cover design by Luke Causby / Blue Cork
Cover photographs courtesy of the Baird family collection
Author photo of Ben Mckelvey courtesy Simon Upton
Typeset in 12/19.8 pt Sabon LT Pro by Bookhouse, Sydney
Printed and bound in Australia by McPherson's Printing Group

THE WARRIOR'S PRAYER

Live your life that the fear of death can never enter your heart. Trouble no one about their religion; respect others in their view, and demand that they respect yours.

Love your life, perfect your life, beautify all things in your life. Seek to make your life long and its purpose in the service of your people.

Prepare a noble death song for the day when you go over the great divide.

Always give a word or a sign of salute when meeting or passing a friend, even a stranger, when in a lonely place. Show respect to all people and grovel to none.

When you arise in the morning give thanks for the joy of living. If you see no reason for giving thanks, the fault lies only in yourself.

Abuse no one and no thing, for abuse turns the wise ones to fools and robs the spirit of its vision.

When it comes your time to die, be not like those whose hearts are filled with the fear of death, so that when their time comes they weep and pray. Sing your death song proudly, and die like a warrior going home.

Tecumseh (1768–1813)

CONTENTS

AUTHOR'S NOTE

There's a hole inside many of the men whom I interviewed for this book. That hole is black and deep and sucking, the edges often crusted with Afghan dust and cordite.

Every war ends; so too every career in the special forces. When peace is unnerving or dull, life is difficult.

Every page after this one is written in the service of remembering Bairdy, but this page is reserved for the restless, incomplete men who live on. Those men, who don't trust promiscuously, were generous with their time and their stories.

They're the reason this books exists, so to them I say thank you, and good luck.

Ben Mckelvey
Sydney, 2017

THE COMING STORM

KHOD VALLEY, AFGHANISTAN
22 JUNE 2013

Jutting, arid mountains sail past the windows of the American Chinook. They're the high ground, the borders of the battlespace, the domain of the scout and the sniper. When the helicopter banks, the valley floor can be seen: green and lush, the centre of Uruzgan life. This is the domain of the Australian Special Forces assault team.

Arrangements of these six-man chalks can smash through the valleys like a tidal wave. To watch them operate is to see a harmony of flanking, covering fire, grenades and relentless advance.

Cameron Baird commands one of these chalks. He can be recognised in the Chinook by his size, and by his immaculately clean M4 assault rifle. Unlike the other matte weapons, his rifle shimmers when the sun flashes into the chopper. His facial paint is unique too. It's not the disrupted pattern that most choose for assaults; Baird prefers to look like a Mohican warrior, or a Day of the Dead reveller. This is a man who wants to be seen by the enemy, and feared.

Baird is not a 'phantom of the jungle', a nickname the enemy gave the Australian Special Air Service Regiment (SASR) in Vietnam for their capacity to disappear and reappear at will. He's a commando, a howling banshee, smashing through the Taliban like a wrecking ball.

A call comes in from the pilot – three minutes to target. Baird's legs vibrate like a bass string. He stretches his arms and neck as though about to run onto the football field. Jack Ducat, another team commander, catches Baird's eye. Cam grins and lets out a whoop.

It's fuckin' on. No dry holes today, no empty compounds. Here, at the very end of Australia's war, the boys are getting one last crack at the shitbirds.

Songs often bounce around in Cam Baird's head during helicopter rides. Quite often songs from AC/DC; songs that were efficient and powerful, riding steadily on three-chord rhythms before changing gears to solos that shrieked around corners and burst over crests. Cam's favourites were about rolling thunder, and pouring rain, shooting to thrill, and playing to kill. A personal favourite was about getting loose from the noose.

The load door opens. The ground approaches. Dust blows into the helicopter.

Sometimes Cam contemplates passages from the books he's been reading, volumes about Eastern spirituality by writers such as Ram Dass.

There has never been a time when you and I have not existed, nor will there be a time when we will cease to exist. As the same person inhabits the body through childhood, youth, and old age, so too at the time of death he attains another body. The wise are not deluded by these changes.

In his quiet hours, Cameron Baird – rum drinker, footy lover and fearsome warrior – is also a philosopher and deep thinker, but this is no quiet hour. His mind is only on the battle ahead.

Boots on the ground, weapon up. So begins the last incredible day of the life of Cameron Baird VC, MG.

CHAPTER ONE

THE FAMILY BAIRD

*'He had ten fingers for handballing and ten toes for
kicking, I thought he looked pretty good to me.'*
DOUG BAIRD

MELBOURNE, VICTORIA
BURNIE, TASMANIA
1964–1987

Doug Baird played footy, and Kaye Stewart danced. In
north-east Melbourne in the late 1960s, that's just what
you did.

It was a different Melbourne from the one we know
now, a smaller, more conservative city. Inexpensive housing
was attainable by the working class, and most jobs were in
manufacturing. The unemployment rate was less than 2 per

cent, bread cost 18 cents a loaf and the British monarchy was deeply loved.

But some things never change. Then, as now, footy was a religion, with nearly 120 000 people (roughly 15 per cent of the population of Melbourne at the time) sometimes cramming into the MCG for VFL games. Footy dominated the papers, radio and TV – when they weren't focused on rock and roll, which had become all the rage after Beatlemania smashed into the city in June 1964.

When Kaye met Doug, he was an outstanding junior footballer heading towards a VFL career. She was a recent graduate of a secretarial college, working during the day and dancing, sometimes competitively, at night. Doug's junior footy was played for Carlton, and the Blues were the club Kaye's family supported, but when the pair met it was on Kaye's turf – the dance floor.

'I had to go to the dances. That's where the girls were,' says Doug. 'Back in those days the girls used to wear miniskirts. I reckon I was attracted to Kaye the first time I saw her legs.'

While Doug speaks of that first meeting, Kaye leans back, a pursed but proud smile on her face. At sixty-seven, Doug Baird still draws himself tall, and I am yet to see Kaye with her hair out of place or her outfit thoughtlessly assembled. They are a handsome couple, and occasionally I see glimpses of the young footballer and the elegant dancer. When in company, Doug speaks more willingly than Kaye, who is more voluble in one-on-one conversations.

Kaye admits she didn't think much of Doug when she first saw him. He was tall and broad for a 17-year-old, and had some cachet because of his football prowess, but he was also nearly two years younger than her, and suffered from an apparently incurable case of two left feet. 'He looked like a big kid to me,' she says.

Doug was persistent, though, and over a number of months – and dances – the pair became familiar, then close, then eventually they fell in love. Even though they weren't yet in their twenties, they knew they would be a pair for life.

'It was different in those days,' Doug says. 'You didn't run around. If you found a good thing, you stuck with it.'

Over three years of courtship, the pair would spend most of their spare time together. Kaye started work at the loans department of a finance company, while Doug qualified as a plumber. Each weekend they ventured to the footy fields of Melbourne, Kaye to cheer and Doug to play.

In 1968, when the couple first met, Doug was a burly, uncompromising full-forward for the Carlton Reserves. On 22 July that year, *The Age* had this to say of the young prospect: 'Doug Baird has not played a senior game with Carlton. However, fans have already got his name on a banner and displayed it among the "big names" on Saturday. Baird recently kicked eight goals for the Reserves. He is considered to have a bright future in League football.'

Later that year, when he turned 18 and became eligible for conscription to Vietnam, it looked as though Doug's bright future in football would have to at least pause. Military conscription at the time was based on randomly chosen birthdates, with men deemed eligible for conscription compelled to go and serve if their birthday came up.

When the unlucky birthdates were announced, they didn't coincide with Doug's. The day before and the day after were chosen, but not his. Doug had no strong feelings about the Vietnam War or communism. He was largely apolitical, but would have gone to fight if he'd been drafted. 'It was the thing you do, you see,' he says. Mainly he was relieved because he wanted to keep going with his footy.

In 1969 Doug Baird played his first senior match for Carlton. With the club's superstar forward, Alex Jesaulenko, out with injury, and other players off on representative duties, Doug was called up for a game against North Melbourne at the Shinboners' home ground, the Arden Street Oval.

'I remember being so excited, and when I ran out I was doing some little sprints, burning off energy,' says Doug. 'I got a set shot near the goal and initially kicked into the man. I remember the crowd. The opposition player had gone over the mark, so I kicked again and got a goal, my first in senior footy.'

Doug kicked two goals that day, and the Blues had a comfortable 21-point win. Kaye was there, cheering her boyfriend on. It was supposed to be the start of a long career in the top league for Doug, but that wasn't to be.

Named as a reserve for three of the next four games, Doug didn't get much playing time, nor was he named in any of the finals teams that year. The next year, 1970, he again played well in the reserves team, but was unable to win a permanent place in the senior side.

Baird played his last game for Carlton a little more than 400 days after his debut, for a total of six senior matches and eight goals. Still only 21, Doug moved to play in the VFA, first for Prahran and then for Brunswick. There he excelled.

Although Doug's footy career wasn't going exactly to plan, his relationship with Kaye was only going from strength to strength. In 1972 the couple married. The maid of honour and bridesmaids were Kaye's sisters, Carole and Heather, and her best friend, Diane, while the groomsmen were Doug's mates, VFL premiership-winning players Robert Walls, Vin Waite and Andy Lukas. The ceremony was a traditionally Presbyterian one, and the reception traditionally Australian. In exceptional heat, literally hundreds of 'king browns' were consumed, prompting Kaye's father to mention to Doug – in awe – how much beer his mates could put away. It fuelled a party that Doug and Kaye say they will never forget.

'It was 35 degrees [Celsius] that day and the air conditioning broke down, but that certainly didn't stop anyone from dancing,' Doug says with a smile.

Once married, Doug's VFA career boomed. During the 1974 season, he kicked 98 goals for Brunswick; the next year he kicked another 95 and won the best and fairest award.

After that, an attractive offer arrived, not from a VFL club, but from a club playing in the Tasmanian Football League (TFL). The Cooee Bulldogs, one of two TFL teams representing the town of Burnie, a small forestry and paper-milling town on the north-west coast of Tasmania, wanted Doug as its marquee player. The club's offer of $200 a game and a $500 signing bonus was a considerable amount of money in the mid-1970s, more than many of Doug's mates were earning in the VFL.

Kaye and Doug had never been to Tasmania, so the club invited them to have a look around the town before they made a decision. They did, and Kaye admits she was less than impressed with the place, her face bunching even now as she thinks back. 'They took us to the famous Burnie lookout,' she says, 'and I was looking out at all the smoke pumping out of the Pulp [the Burnie Paper Mill], and I thought, *What a horrible place.* They showed us some houses and I hated those too.'

Doug and Kaye decided to take up the offer anyway. Kaye was pregnant with their first child, and Doug wanted to play professional footy. They were still in their early twenties, and reasoned that as long as they were together, it didn't really matter where they lived. They planned to stay in Burnie for a few years, and when Doug stopped playing football they would go back to Melbourne. That was Doug's promise to Kaye.

'We were young and we really didn't have anything to lose,' Kaye recalls.

Four months before they moved to Tasmania, Kaye gave birth to their first child, a boy they named Brendan Lindsay Baird.

The town's two teams – the Cooee Bulldogs and the Burnie Tigers – were the social lifeblood of the remote town, and people went out of their way to get to know the Bulldogs' star import and his pretty young wife. The local women and girls were more than happy to help Kaye with her house and baby, and Doug, a third-generation hunter and outdoorsman, was quickly welcomed into a community of shooters, divers and fishermen. They made friends quickly.

Just like footy clubs everywhere, the Bulldogs looked after their own. The club helped the young family out with a loan so Doug could start his own plumbing business, and they funnelled jobs his way to get him going. The footy club did everything possible to keep the Bairds happy and Doug playing well, and in the Tasmanian league he almost always played well.

After Doug, Kaye and Brendan had been in Burnie for two years, an economic slowdown in the town stymied the local building industry, and Doug's plumbing business stalled. The club stepped up again, helping Doug change careers by organising a job for him at a local Ford dealership, where he took up selling Falcons, Meteors and F-100 pick-up trucks.

'I didn't know anything about selling cars,' Doug says, 'but people would come by to get their photo taken with me and I'd tell them about the cars – what I knew about them, anyway. The people at the shop saw value in it.

Things were really great in Burnie for a long time. We couldn't really have asked for much more.'

'Things were going so well we decided to have another baby,' Kaye adds.

Cameron Stewart Baird was born on a cold, squally afternoon in June 1981 at North West Regional Hospital. The new baby arrived 'as punctual as a good soldier', says Doug, who at the time was playing footy at West Park Oval, just down the road from the hospital.

While Brendan had been born by Caesarean section, Cam's birth was natural, and onerous.

'When they brought him to me I just said, "Take him away." I'd had enough of it all,' remembers Kaye. 'A girl-friend was with me and she said, "He's so beautiful," but I said, "How can you say that? He's the ugliest baby I've ever seen. He's so wrinkly."'

After such an intense labour, Kaye initially had trouble bonding with Cam in hospital. Doug was enamoured with Cameron from the moment he laid eyes on him. 'When I saw he had ten fingers for handballing and ten toes for kicking, I thought he looked pretty good to me,' he says.

That day, Doug was thinking, he had just doubled his chances of having another footy star in the house.

—

Doug Baird played 130 games for Cooee, and after he retired as a player, he stayed in the TFL as a coach. With a baby and a pre-schooler in the house, and support around her, Kaye was happy in Burnie for the time being, but Doug's promise that the pair would one day move back to Melbourne was never far from her thoughts.

'My sisters were having babies [in Melbourne], and the weather wasn't great in Tasmania,' she says. 'As Cameron grew up, I started bringing it up more and more with Doug. Most of the jobs in the town were at the paper mill, and I wanted more than that for my boys.'

'Kaye was right,' Doug adds. 'It seemed like the best thing to do for the kids. I was still a bit famous in Burnie – footy had made me a big fish in a very small pond. As I got older, I felt like some of that was rubbing off onto Brendan. We just thought a bit of anonymity might do us good.'

Brendan was nine years old and Cameron was three-and-a-half when Doug made good on his promise and the family headed back to Melbourne. They settled in Gladstone Park, a northern suburb close to the airport.

There, Doug started a career in building sales in Melbourne, and also began coaching VFA side Northcote. He even played a little more in the VFA himself, but he was no longer the firebrand forward he had once been, having lost a step of pace and a few degrees of competitive heat.

Doug played his last match of footy in 1987, just in time for Brendan and Cam to take over the big league dream. The elder Baird boy would find, however, that footy wasn't his passion. The younger, like his father, would find that it's a dream that can be elusive.

CHAPTER TWO

THE BOY

*'A small bird will drop frozen dead from a bough
without ever having felt sorry for itself.'*

'SELF-PITY', D.H. LAWRENCE

MELBOURNE, VICTORIA
1986–2000

Cameron Baird started school in 1986 at Gladstone Views
Primary. It was a typical Melbourne suburban primary
school. At lunchtime the sounds of the children playing
would be silenced by planes going to and from Tullamarine
and Essendon airports, which were a couple of kilometres
west and south, respectively.

Even in prep school, Cam was known as a physical
boy who loved to test the limits of his athleticism. When

16

he hit Year One, Kaye went along to the school for a regular parent/teacher night and was surprised to be told that Cameron was too competitive and too singular in his focus, which was often on something other than his schoolwork. The teacher suspected this would be a lifelong problem, and said Kaye should not expect him 'to amount to too much in life'.

'Those were [the teacher's] exact words. I remember it very well,' says Kaye. 'I walked away in a daze. I knew my boy, and he was such a good kid. I just thought, *Stuff her – she can think what she wants, but she's wrong.*'

Throughout primary school Cam established himself as a middling scholar but an exceptional athlete. A large and powerful child, he found that each year he could run faster and jump further than any of his contemporaries, and the gap between his physical abilities and those of his peers seemed only to be widening. By Year Four Cameron was bigger than almost any other child at the school. By Year Five he was bigger than most of the teachers.

While Cameron's competitive drive never dimmed in his life, when he was around eight or nine years old it seemed to turn inward; after that he only ever considered he was in competition with himself. He was never known for bragging or exaggerating. Even as a child, the competitiveness that was a defining characteristic for Cam was never used to belittle or diminish others.

In his latter years at primary school, Cameron rarely celebrated his regular wins at school athletics events. Doug says he would usually give away his athletics medals and ribbons to the other kids.

'It was weird seeing a kid not really showing emotion after winning stuff,' Doug recalls. 'It was almost as though he was waiting for a test that he thought was worthy of celebrating.'

Cam's older brother, Brendan, was also a big and athletic child – larger than Cameron – but says that he never had the self-discipline or desire for success that his younger brother had. He never pushed himself like Cam did. At Little Athletics competitions, Cam's prowess eventually became embarrassing for Brendan, who would find himself finishing in the middle of the pack while Cam was usually winning. Sometimes girls asked Brendan why he wasn't as good as his little brother.

Being compared unfavourably to your younger sibling is tough, and by his early teens Brendan had had enough. He stopped going to Little Athletics, and would refuse to let his parents and brother attend his team sports matches. Brendan sometimes lashed out and teased his little brother about being a 'two-headed Tasmanian', but Doug and Kaye say Cam rarely took the bait, and rarely fought with his brother. Some of Cam's mates have suggested that, even at a very young age, he understood Brendan's frustration and did all he could not to exacerbate it.

From the time when Cam was big enough to put shoes on, Doug started taking him down to the park to teach him how to kick a football. Almost as soon as he could talk, Cam was rabbiting on to anyone who would listen about Stephen Kernahan or Fraser Brown or Adrian Gleeson or Stephen Silvagni or any other Carlton player of the period. That pleased Doug, and amused Kaye.

Cam was always up for a trip to Princes Park or Windy Hill when there was a game on, and when there wasn't he would be trying to get Brendan, Doug or one of his mates to go and kick the footy at the Jack Ginifer Reserve, across the road from his primary school. Kaye wouldn't let Cam play in any organised football competitions until he was eight, but as soon as he was old enough, Cameron dedicated himself to Aussie Rules, body and soul.

Cam played other team sports and continued in athletics – he even became junior Australian discus and shot-put champion – but from the day he pulled on a football jersey, his greatest love was always the Australian game. It quickly became apparent to anyone watching that Cameron had a preternatural aptitude for the sport.

—

Gladstone Views Primary School was the first post for a young teacher named Andrew Harrison, so when he was asked to coach the footy team, he said yes straightaway, despite a complete lack of coaching and playing experience. He'd watched a lot of footy – surely that counted for something.

The school team was traditionally farmed from Years Five and Six, but at the team's first training sessions, Harrison found that there were fewer bodies than jerseys. If he was going to field a team, he was going to have to start recruiting. When he told a fellow teacher about his predicament, he was told about an exceptionally large fourth-grader named Cameron Baird, who could usually be found playing with his mates in the quadrangle.

Harrison took Cam aside and asked him if he played footy. Cam said he did: he'd just started playing modified-rules junior games for club side Gladstone Park. Would he be interested in playing for the school as well, Harrison wanted to know. Cam said he was – 'but first you have to talk to my mum'. It was a short season, so Kaye approved.

After a few training sessions, Cameron established himself as a formidable force in the ruck. Soon, a nine-year-old Cam Baird was leading a Gladstone Views team made up entirely of older students onto the field.

'He wasn't pushing for it, either,' Harrison says. 'He had Year Five and Year Six kids pushing him forward to lead them out. As someone who's now spent decades working in primary schools, that is really, really strange stuff.'

Gladstone Views played six games after Cameron joined, winning 'a few of them', according to Harrison's recollection.

When Cam went back to school the next year, he strode up to Andrew Harrison and told him that he'd spent the summer working on his game with his dad. He was going to be better and the team was going to do a lot better that year too.

'Well, that's nice,' Harrison replied.

Harrison says the improvement in Cam and in the team was drastic. He'd been a big kid with a competitive streak, but now he understood the game. This was the year, the teacher says, that he started assuming Cam was destined to play top-level football.

At the end of the season Cameron was the 26th player picked for the 25-player Victorian primary schoolboys side. The coaches relayed to Harrison the message that the boy had only missed out because he lacked some penetration with his left boot, and because his handballing on his left side was weaker too. Cam knew what he had to work on.

During the next summer, Cam and his father spent literally hundreds of hours in ambidexterity drills. Once again, Cam arrived at school on day one of the new year and announced to Harrison that his game had improved.

'He asked me if we could go to the Jack Ginifer Reserve so he could show me how good he was with his left boot now,' the teacher says. 'I called Kaye, she said it was okay and off we went. His skills were amazing. So much better. He could kick a goal from the square with his left and his right, and he was getting even bigger and stronger. I couldn't wait for the footy season.'

Photographs of Cam with his schoolmates that year are extraordinary. So much larger than all of the other boys, Cameron could almost be a parent or older brother, were it not for his innocent, childish face, which beams out of the pictures with a smile too big even for his oversized body.

Before the footy season that year, Cam played in the Gladstone Views cricket team as an all-rounder. At the season's start, Harrison, then the vice-president of the Victorian School Sports Association, suggested to his peers that the Kookaburra Commander, the ball set to be used for games that year, should be replaced with a softer ball, lest someone be injured by his giant young fast bowler.

The idea was ignored. When the season was only three games old, and Cameron had been witnessed smashing batsmen and wickets alike around north-west Melbourne, an extraordinary meeting of the association was convened to ratify Harrison's suggestion.

'When he wasn't playing, he was very gentle, especially with smaller kids, and was really aware of his size and strength, but when he was playing sports he was very . . . competitive,' Harrison says.

When the footy season started, Cam dominated most of the games he played in. On more than one occasion aggrieved parents and teachers from opposing teams asked to see his birth certificate, because they couldn't quite believe that a child so young could be so good and so large.

Playing out of the ruck, Cam could usually grab the ball from the bounce, run forward and kick as many goals as were required for victory.

'We could have won most of our games by 100 points that year,' Harrison says, 'but Cam was actually the one that decided we should have some rules to make the game fairer for the opposition, and more enjoyable for his teammates.'

These rules included Cam kicking the ball to the first Gladstone Views jersey he saw after getting the ball out of the ruck – but only after the team had built up a four- or five-goal lead.

Despite being a particularly top-heavy team, Gladstone Views went to the semi-final of the Victorian schools' championships. That game was played in torrential rain, on a pitch that looked like a Western Front battlefield. At three-quarter time, Harrison's side was down by four goals – a considerable margin in a very low scoring affair. Harrison took Cam aside and told him that the only way the team would win was if he could provide an exceptional individual effort. It was Cameron's moment to do it all, and Gladstone Views ended up winning the match by a point. They would lose the grand final by four goals, but that semi-final win was something Cameron and his friends considered so special.

That year, Cameron Baird was named captain of a state schoolboys side that included Jonathan Brown (who would go on to captain the Brisbane Lions) and led Victoria to a national championship – something the state hadn't managed for a decade. It was one of many accolades that would be conferred on Cam during his footy career, but he always maintained that Gladstone Views' semi-final win was the greatest moment of his footy life.

Cameron had a close group of friends from primary school until he joined the Army. When asked why that particular moment had been so special to him, almost to a man they said it was because they shared it together. Although Cameron Baird was usually the reason they won, *they* were the reason he remembered winning so fondly. From an early age, it seems, Cam had a great interest in how friendship and leadership could be fused for best effect.

Doug had spent that bitter-cold semi-final close to Cam, positioning himself next to the goal that his son was attacking. Cameron's footy career would continue for another decade or so after that, and Doug usually arranged his working week around Cameron's training and matches so that he could support his son. He lived and died every mark and every kick with Cam.

'I loved the way Cameron played footy,' Doug says. 'Although Cam played up front, like I did, he had such a different type of game to mine. Cam didn't have the shit in him. I'd stomp on people and swing arms, and got rubbed out [suspended] pretty regularly, but that just wasn't Cam. He was always a happy and very fair player. I reckon I was getting as much joy out of it as he was, because it was all so different to the way I played footy.'

Andrew Harrison agrees. 'On the field he was as hard and courageous a kid as I'd ever seen,' he says. 'But he was just so mature, too. A kid that powerful has the capability to be difficult, but Cam was always thinking of the other kids and was never, ever resented. The best players I ever saw at that age were the Selwood brothers and Cameron.'

Since he first coached the Gladstone Views team, Andrew Harrison has been continuously involved in junior football, and the walls of his office are laden with memorabilia. One piece that hangs larger than the others is a framed jersey of orange and green, alongside an image of an oversized sixth-grader named Cameron.

—

Footy may have been his first love, but at ten-and-a-half Cameron Baird found another. Doug still had a lot of old football contacts in Melbourne, and from time to time he would be invited to attend games and concerts. On one occasion Doug asked Cam if he wanted to go and see AC/DC with him at the Melbourne Tennis Centre. Cam had never heard of AC/DC, but from the first chord of the first song of the band's Razors Edge concert, he was spellbound. So began a love that would endure for his whole life.

After that October 1991 concert, Doug and Kaye bought Cameron a guitar and for the first time footy had to share his obsessive affections. Kaye says that there was rarely a day that Cam didn't practise; she remembers being surprised at the concentration and dedication Cam gave to his guitar playing. There were few weekends when he didn't kick the footy or play his guitar – or both.

Doug still loved to head out to the bush to shoot, fish and camp, and he'd usually take his father, John Baird. By the time Brendan and Cam were old enough to go too, John was not a particularly well man. He was suffering a number of ailments, including some he'd developed after being exposed to a chemical weapons test in north Queensland at the start of World War II.

Although he couldn't always participate in the hunting, John relished the trips with his son and grandsons and would find other ways to be useful. Often John would be confined to the camp while Doug and the boys set out fishing, or hunting for pig or deer, but he was more than happy gutting and skinning the caught animals, and making sure there was a hot meal ready when the others returned.

'Cam really loved my dad,' Doug says, 'and would hang on every word when my old man would tell stories.'

Occasionally John would talk about his experiences in the Second Australian Imperial Force (2nd AIF). Once he told the boys about the combat he saw in the Pacific campaign, when the 2nd AIF was augmenting the US Army units commanded by General Douglas MacArthur in the New Guinea campaign in 1945, near the end of the war.

John Baird's unit was pinned down by Japanese machine-gunners, and John was tasked with charging a pillbox and lobbing a grenade in through the gun slit. After getting the grenade in, John ran away, only to find the grenade landing at his feet, having been thrown back by the Japanese gunners. He had just enough time to hurl the grenade back in the direction of the Japanese before diving for cover.

Doug says Cam cherished that story, but it was because he loved his grandfather, not because he relished war stories. Cam was never a boy who played at being a soldier or dreamed of battlefield heroics. He didn't play with toy guns either. For him, guns were always a tool, not a prop of boyhood fantasy. Cam's youthful dreams all revolved around rock music and footy.

Andrew Harrison remembers taking Cameron's Year Six class to Canberra so they could visit the Australian War Memorial. Cam was particularly interested in the Roll of Honour, the commemorative area in the middle of the memorial where the names of the Australians killed while serving in the armed forces since 1885 are recorded in brass lettering.

'He was really interested in what might have happened to all the people, all the names,' Harrison says. 'He was especially interested in how difficult it must have been for each of them, how brave many of them must have been, and what it might have been like in their final moment.'

As Cameron moved into his teenage years, he increasingly saw a future for himself in football. Back when the family lived in Tasmania, Brendan had developed an obsession with Wynyard Airport, riding his bike there every day after school to watch the planes take off and land; now, in Melbourne, he would tell his little brother about how he was going to work at the airport one day, even if it was handling baggage or working in a concession. Whenever Brendan asked his little brother what he wanted to do, the answer was always the same: 'Footy player.'

Had Cam grown up anywhere else, he might have been discouraged from putting all his eggs in such an unlikely basket, but in Gladstone Park professional football was seen as an admirable goal. Everyone couldn't wait to be mates with a famous footy player.

'When we got to high school, he still did his work, but he wasn't putting a lot into school,' says Chris Dyer, Cameron's best and most enduring friend before he joined the Army. 'He was liked by the teachers and never got in any trouble, but Cam was going to be in the AFL. We knew it, and the teachers knew it, and everyone was pretty happy about that.'

Dyer's teenage growth spurt came later than for some others, and with Cam being a giant from the outset they were a funny-looking duo. Dyer was Cam's mate though, and to Cam that meant everything. Despite his size, therefore, Chris Dyer went through his school years with no possibility of being bullied.

Footy, mates and music were the pulses of Cameron Baird's high-school life. When I visited Gladstone Park high school the teachers remembered him fondly as the big kid who could usually be found in the quadrangle, happily having a game of downball or playing his guitar with his shorts rolled up. (One time, a substitute teacher took Cam's guitar away from him and banned him from playing in the quad, earning a lifelong enemy.) Of course, there were a few necessary trips into the classroom in between. Cam's teachers said that in class he was present and respectful, but not particularly applied. Cam wasn't a bad student – he was just disinterested, happy to do the minimum. Passing was enough for him, as long as he excelled on the footy pitch.

Cam had the rebel in him, but only ever for a real cause. While the other kids were smoking and drinking to prove their teenage bona fides, Cam would always decline. The boys were also regular scrappers, fighting in school or down at the shops.

'We'd be out getting in fights and getting pissed but he wasn't interested in that,' says Rick Green, a close high-school friend. 'I'd be telling him about a big night out and dust-ups and he'd look at me, and I could see it in his eyes. He was like, "Don't be such a dickhead. You're getting nothing out of this."'

Scrapping might have been a regular occurrence in the neighbourhood, but Cam was only ever involved in two fights, and both times was coming to the defence of mates who were being beaten.

'He was so big, there was just no glory in it for him so he didn't bother,' says Chris. 'We hit that age where we'd be shits, but he was just very even. He was always just there getting ready to play AFL footy. We'd eat crap, and he'd be there, ripping up a bread roll and sticking a banana in there.'

Cam wasn't that interested in girlfriends then either, as they required time he could otherwise pour into his footy. Every conversation and every action was about footy, footy and footy.

'Brendan was six-foot-five and a massive kick of the footy, but he just didn't develop the drive Cam had,' says Len Hannah, then a coach of the Calder Cannons and a teacher of both Baird brothers at high school. 'That's no slight on Brendan either, but Cam's ticker set him apart from almost all the other guys I coached.'

—

Cam had been playing his junior footy at Gladstone Park, but when he was 14 the Cannons, a premier AFL feeder club, started showing interest in him. He was too young to join the side, but the club indicated they had an interest in the burly forward and suggested he move from Gladstone Park, which was playing in a B-grade competition, to the A-grade Strathmore.

After one season at Strathmore – in which he broke his arm midway through the season but still won the best and fairest – Cam was tapped to join the Calder Cannons in the TAC Cup, the premier under-18 competition in the country.

The Cannons at the time were known as 'the Football Factory' due to the number of their players who had progressed to the AFL. The late 1990s group in which Cameron Baird found himself included some of the great footballers of the next decade and a half, including Paul Chapman and Jude Bolton. Coaches Len Hannah and Robert Hyde say Cameron was, at that stage, as good as any of them.

Bolton, a two-time AFL premiership player with the Sydney Swans, says he was impressed by Cam as soon as he started playing with him. 'He was one of those guys you'd go into battle with,' he recalls. 'He was extremely courageous.'

'He always made you feel part of the group,' says Andrew Welsh, who went on to play 160 games for Essendon. Two years younger than Cam, Welsh looked up to him. 'Even though you were young and had a lot to learn, his compassion towards the younger guys was something unheard of.'

Baird was often quiet off the pitch, but when he committed to a conversation it's because he had something to say. Cam could often make other players laugh, with a sense of humour so deadpan one could question whether he was part of a joke at all.

Speaking to News Limited, two-time premiership winning Geelong player David Johnson remembers one late afternoon before training when Baird seemed unusually distant. Cam was spinning a ball in his hands close to his face, and he was lost in his thoughts. Johnson was concerned. He asked Cam if he was okay. After another few spins of the ball, Cam spoke.

'Johnno, one day I will bring out a perfume called Sherrin.' Baird stopped spinning the ball and took a long sniff of the football. 'If a woman smelled like a Sherrin, I wouldn't be able to keep my hands off her.'

'This huge smile came across his face,' Johnson said. 'It still makes me laugh.'

Life for Cam happened between the first and final sirens of each match. On the field, he started developing skills that would become vital in his later vocation. Cam's size made him good, but everyone who knew him at this time spoke about his love of teamwork, and his dedication to his teammates. One only had to put on the same jersey as Cameron and he'd treat you like family.

But while Cam would do anything for you, that privilege came with responsibility. Len Hannah remembers an instance when the Cannons were playing in Queensland, and he couldn't get the best out of one of his star players, Paul Chapman. After a half of footy the team was flagging; the immensely talented Chapman had been largely absent.

On the way to the rooms, the then 15-year-old Cam took his adult coach aside, telling him to give Chapman a bollocking. 'If you put a big firecracker in his arse, he'll respond,' Cam said.

Hannah did, and Chapman, who would go on to play in three AFL premierships for Geelong, did respond, winning the game for the Cannons almost single-handedly. 'In the rooms after, Cam was practically smirking,' Hannah remembers.

As far as everyone in junior footy was concerned, both Chapman and Bolton were destined for careers in the AFL, but so too was Cameron Baird.

Bolton says he fully expected Cam to become not only an AFL player, but also a great. 'The marquee key forward at that stage was probably Wayne Carey, arguably one of the greatest players at that time. I think I envisaged him as the next Wayne Carey,' says Bolton.

'He was very Wayne Carey–like,' Chapman agrees. 'He had that waddle and was very strong above his head.'

Over the last two years of Cameron Baird's time at school, AFL clubs starting informing him that they were planning on drafting him when he became eligible. Representatives from the Adelaide Crows visited the house, while Geelong sent a letter saying that Cam would likely be one of their draft picks.

Then, in his last year of junior footy, Cam was playing in a practice match and suffered a relatively serious injury. An opposing player came over the top of Cam in a contest, and he felt acute pain in his shoulder as he tumbled to the ground. He was taken to hospital and told that his shoulder required surgery. He'd be out of action for a number of weeks.

'When that happened we thought it was just a bump in the road,' says Chris Dyer. 'We were kids then. If your arm doesn't actually fall off it isn't going to stop you from doing anything. He had his arm in the sling for a bit. Had his operation and we thought, *Away we go*.'

After his recovery period, Cam continued to train as though he would, the next year, be suiting up for AFL games. He gave no indication that his shoulder injury had affected his capabilities. In preparation for being drafted, he started working with Hannah not only on his skills but also on his strength and fitness.

Cam told his friends that he was a little concerned about his speed, especially his first step of pace. Observers started to compare him to a contemporary, Cameron Ling. Both young men dominated their games, but neither was seen as an explosive, fast-twitch runner. Hearing that Ling was going to a specialist speed coach to improve that deficiency, Cam thought he should do the same.

'I did this level three coaching course in Watsonia and I met this really top-line strength and conditioning guy, so I got Cam to go and see this bloke,' says Hannah. 'He took Cam through a range of different exercises that were concentrating on power and speed, rather than beach muscles. If anything, they were to make him a bit smaller and more agile.'

Part of the reason Cam had dominated junior footy was because he had such a size advantage, but Hannah knew that would be diminished, if not negated completely, when he started playing in the AFL.

'I'd talk to recruiters,' the coach recalls, 'and they would always be talking about making sure they didn't get guys who are too big. We want them this size, this shape. We needed to be careful not to do too much heavy leg work. I told him that once, and he cracked the shits. He said, "Fuck it, mate, I am what I am. I don't want to spend my whole life impressing other people." An outburst like that was uncharacteristic, but I was pretty impressed and I thought, *You're right, mate.*'

It was around this time that Len Hannah started to think that Cameron might not be drafted in 1999. The shoulder injury had happened at a very inopportune moment, and perhaps hadn't left enough time for Cam to clear away the clouds over his speed. Hannah didn't articulate this to anyone, hoping he would be proved wrong. Even if he wasn't, he had no doubt that Cam would either join a rookie list or be picked up the following year.

After completing Year 12, Cam joined his mates on a schoolies camping trip to Torquay. On their first night away, two of his friends polished off a bottle of vodka. Cam took the empty bottle and for the rest of the trip drank water from it, in this way heading off any questions about why he wasn't imbibing like everyone else.

A few weeks later, the 1999 AFL national draft came around. Doug and Kaye's place was just down the road from the school. With a pool out the front, it had always been a hangout for many of Brendan's and Cameron's mates. Now they all assembled there to watch Cam (and Doug's) AFL dream come true.

After eating snags and steaks cooked by Doug on the barbecue, a dozen or so of Cam's family and mates crowded around the television. Cam, who was wearing his best jeans, shirt and black leather shoes, sat and waited to hear his name read out. He had been told that Geelong was the club most interested, with Adelaide second. A few other dark horses had expressed interest, but the most likely candidates were definitely the Cats and the Crows.

Geelong's first pick was at eight, and they used it to select Western Australian Joel Corey. Geelong then picked at 15, 17, 23 and 31. Among their choices were two of Cam's teammates from the Calder Cannons, Ezra Bray and Paul Chapman. By now Geelong had picked up five players, but not the one whose name the group crowding around a television in Gladstone Park desperately wanted to hear. The tension grew thick.

Adelaide took its first pick at thirty-six. They selected a local player. The group in Gladstone Park was silent until Geelong's next pick.

'At 38, Geelong picks Cameron –'

The room erupted in cheers. Everyone was out of their seats, ready to embrace Cam.

'– Ling.'

Silence. They all sat back down, except for Cam, who said nothing. Eventually he walked to the door and jogged off down the street. By the time he returned, sweaty and exhausted, his friends had left. Doug asked if he wanted to talk, but he didn't.

Cam Baird's life had been leading up to this one moment, but it had become one of crushing disappointment. Now this young man of singular focus had absolutely no idea what to do the next day, let alone the next week or for the rest of his life.

—

A couple of AFL clubs approached Cam after the draft, suggesting he should go and play reserves footy and nominate for the draft again the next year. Cam said he wasn't interested. A few VFL clubs made offers, and Cam turned those down too. He wouldn't even enter a conversation about football with most of his mates.

'The one thing that blows my mind is that, given Cam's personality and his drive, why he didn't try again,' Chris Dyer says. 'That's a question I can't answer.'

Len Hannah also tried to talk Cam into trying again in the 2000 national draft. Hannah had been part of a team that had seen no fewer than four players recruited after the 1999 season, and he told Cam he thought he could have the best career of all of them. But Cam wouldn't listen.

Later, Cam would tell friends that he felt like he'd been sold a lie. Not only had people told him that he was destined for the AFL, but they'd said he could be a generational talent. Cam had never rested on those laurels, either. Comments like those had only pushed him to work harder, and now, when it was time for that harvest of training and perseverance to be reaped, there were no returns.

'If the AFL doesn't want me, then I don't want to be part of it,' he told Len Hannah.

'I thought it was a huge waste of a great talent, but he had made up his mind,' the coach remembers.

That left the question of what Cameron Baird was going to do next. Unlike Brendan, who had always wanted to work at the airport, and Cam's schoolmates, who had moved on to trades or further studies, Cam had never even considered a backup career. Then, four days after the draft, inspiration came, courtesy of Ridley Scott and Demi Moore.

G.I. Jane is an American action film in which Jordan O'Neil (Demi Moore) attempts to become the first woman to become a soldier in the US Navy Combined Reconnaissance Team, the movie's equivalent of the US Navy SEALs. The film depicts the extreme trials of SEAL selection, and culminates in the recruits being called up to participate in a special forces raid in Libya.

The overarching theme of the film is self-reliance, self-control and self-belief, and it ends with Demi Moore's character being given a book of poems by D.H. Lawrence. One, entitled 'Self-pity', is circled, and is read out to end the film.

I never saw a wild thing
sorry for itself.
A small bird will drop frozen dead from a bough
without ever having felt sorry for itself.

The day after watching the film, Cam Baird went to a recruitment office and joined the Australian Army.

It was a surprise to all in Cam's life. Brendan had previously been in the Army Reserves, and Cam had always been interested in what he did on the base, but Cam had never so much as suggested he might join the armed forces. He had been a predictable young man in many ways, and everything he'd done in his young life had been in pursuit of a footy career. Even though Cam had said he'd forsaken his football dream after not being drafted, few believed it. Now he was committing to at least four years away from the game, which pretty much meant the AFL was no longer a possibility.

At some point along the way, though, Cam's AFL dream had become not just about him: it had picked up a momentum of its own, driven by friends and coaches and family. Although Doug hadn't pushed Cam, and would have supported him no matter what he chose to do, there was no doubt he would have been the proudest man in the stands when Cam inevitably, or so it seemed, took to the field to play his first AFL game. But joining the Army was Cam's choice, and his alone.

It was only later that Cam's friends and family started to realise that the career he had chosen was an ideal one for him. He would be away from home, and away from Melbourne. No one in the Army would know about his AFL aspirations – in fact, few ever knew that he had played footy – and no one would be asking him what he'd be doing next.

Cam signed his papers, did his physical, shaved his head and waited to find out when he would start his basic training. Then a letter came in the mail: the Australian Army regretted to inform Cam that he was unfit for selection. He had failed the physical. It was his shoulder.

'They don't even want me for the Army,' Cam said to Kaye.

This was one of the few times in his life that Cameron Baird seemed completely uneasy and off-kilter. He stayed morose and angry for two days, and then decided he was going to fight the decision.

Cam went back to the recruiter who had filed his written documentation and argued that there was no reason he couldn't perform the same tasks as any other recruit. Cam filed a dispute and, shortly afterwards, received another letter from the Army. This time it said the official ruling had been overturned, and that Cameron Stewart Baird should report to the local recruitment centre for induction on 4 January 2000.

Cam would never play organised football again. He wasn't a footy player anymore; he was a grunt.

CHAPTER THREE

THE SOLDIER'S CHOICE

'I don't think he was ever destined to be an AFL
player. That bloke was a soldier, through and through.'

PETER EISEN

WAGGA WAGGA, NEW SOUTH WALES
SINGLETON, NEW SOUTH WALES
HOLSWORTHY, NEW SOUTH WALES
2000

In 1947 a US Army military historian, S.L.A. Marshall, made a name for himself when he published a controversial book called *Men Against Fire: The Problem of Battle Command in Future War*. It claimed that most American infantrymen in World War II were largely ineffective.

44

Marshall claimed that 'in an average day's action, the number [of US soldiers] engaging with any and all weapons was approximately 15 per cent'. Further, he claimed that many of the soldiers who did shoot deliberately fired away from the enemy.

Marshall's methodology has been questioned by modern military historians, but the premise of his work – that many men cannot kill unless in extreme mortal danger – remains valid. These men don't make very good infantry soldiers, as generally the purpose of infantry soldiers is to kill the enemy.

A modern Marshall acolyte, Lieutenant Colonel Dave Grossman (US Army retired) says that when an infantry-man is faced with battle, there are four options available to them: they can fight, pretend to fight, run away or surrender. Grossman has written extensively about how infantry training has been revolutionised since World War II, in order to ensure that the modern soldier chooses the first option.

That training includes the firing of real weapons with real ammunition in realistic scenarios against human-like targets. An adherence to extreme obedience is to be fostered too, and – just as important as any other aspect of training – an unwavering fealty to one's fellow grunts. An infantry soldier who will kill and die for the safety of their team, regardless of any personal feelings about them, the platoon, the company or the unit, is an effective soldier.

It was in this modern training environment that Cameron Baird found himself when he reported to the Army Recruit Training Centre, at Kapooka, New South Wales, in January 2000.

Just outside Wagga Wagga, in the south of the state, Kapooka is like a huge Christian youth camp, but instead of dormitories there are barracks. Volleyball courts are replaced by rifle ranges, and discipline, not the word of God, rules.

Cameron had shared the coach ride from central Melbourne with some other recruits. As the bus entered the grounds, they saw a boulder at the gates, with gold capital letters beside a crossed-rifles insignia: 'SOLDIERING BEGINS HERE'.

Of all the aspects of life at Kapooka, most say the initial discipline is the most jarring, and the first couple of weeks, by design, are the most restrictive. When building a modern soldier, the Australian Defence Force (ADF) prefers to start from a somewhat razed foundation, so in their early days at Kapooka the recruits can do no right. No matter how they make their beds, clean their bathrooms or fold their uniforms, they will have done it incorrectly. There will be punishments, and very loud vocal objections at their ineptitude. They are not permitted to contact their family or friends for the first week, though they are encouraged to write letters to loved ones back home.

Cameron Baird had a particularly tough time in his first few days, and many say the reason he found it such hard going was because of the gifts that made him a formidable warrior later in life. As ever, Bairdy was bigger and stronger than most of the other recruits, so he stood out and became a lightning rod for the instructors' confected ire.

In Cam's first phone call home to his parents from Kapooka, it was obvious he was suffering an extreme case of culture shock. In a letter that arrived soon after he wrote, 'I've only been here a few days and so far I hate it,' Cam said. 'The men in charge are real arseholes. The first night I was laying in bed thinking, "what the hell have I got myself into?"' In this letter, Baird complimented the meals ('which is pretty much all you can eat') and the company ('after this shit, I reckon some are going to be my best mates'), but the rest of the letter contained a litany of complaints.

This is all part of ADF strategy. After an initial burst of harsh discipline, recruits are allowed to progress their skills, and to take pride in their development. This is when Cam began to feel a love of soldiering that rarely dampened ever after.

Another letter sent to Doug and Kaye a couple of weeks after his first phone call revealed a dramatically different recruit. Cam wrote that he was now loving Kapooka, and couldn't wait to start 'grunt training'.

Cam described his first experience with the Austeyr rifle, the regular infantry weapon of the ADF, as well as a simulation exercise in which recruits took wounded soldiers off the battlefield, and various fitness tests. He was most excited about being named the 2IC (second-in-command) of his platoon.

'I think this is what I needed,' he wrote. 'I was sick of following, and now I can lead.'

Later in the same letter, Cam had a dig at what he jokingly called 'drug smoking civilian scum' – which, it seemed, included everyone around his age who wasn't a recruit or already in the Army.

Even though he was less than three weeks divorced from civilian life, Cameron said he was very happy that he wasn't 'just hanging around, enjoying the summer, going to the pub'. He wrote about how excited he was at finding a new purpose: being a 'soldier in the greatest army in the world'.

'You now [sic] the old saying, "everything happens for a reason?" Well, I was never put on this earth to play football or anything else, I was meant to be a soldier.'

This sentiment appeared in subsequent letters too — Cam stated, for instance, that he was disappointed when the recruits were allowed to change back into their civilian clothes for a night out. In the same letter he wondered if, after basic training, he would have anything in common with his civilian mates.

This concern was not without reason. Of his own volition, Cameron Baird had chosen to change his life, and it would continue to change as the years went on. His focus was about soldiering now, completely and wholly, and while he would eventually recover an appreciation of his high-school mates, in these early years he came to feel he had little in common with them. Instead, Cam became very close to a few men in his recruit platoon, some of whom would join him in the commando unit. (One remains in Perth, serving with the SASR.)

Cameron Baird graduated from Kapooka on 18 February 2000, and at the March Out Parade, to Doug and Kaye's immense pleasure and surprise, he was named Most Outstanding Soldier in his platoon. (Since 2016, this honour has been renamed the Cameron Baird VC, MG Award.) After Kapooka, Cameron moved to Singleton, north of Sydney, for infantry training.

The ADF has more than 75 000 people on staff, making it one of Australia's largest employers, and while tens of thousands of these roles are held by administrators, doctors, mechanics, cooks, photographers and technicians, the most iconic role has always been that of the infantry soldier. On its website, the ADF describes the infantry as the 'primary combat arm of the Australian Army. The role of the Infantry is to seek out and close with the enemy, to kill or capture him, to seize and hold ground, repel attack, by day or by night, regardless of season, weather or terrain.'

Even though Cam had been named the most outstanding soldier during recruit training, it was in the more realistic scenarios of infantry training that he really started to show what kind of field soldier he would become.

'No one could keep up with him,' says Pete Eisen, an infantryman who became one of Cam's close friends. 'Physically he was streets ahead of everyone, but it was his passion for it that made him something else. If there was any downtime everyone else was happy to get on the piss, but he'd usually be working on his kit or going over exercises.'

During grunt training, recruits were allowed to take the weekends off, and Pete, who would later work with Cam in the commando unit, did try to get him off the base and into the rough nightlife of Newcastle from time to time.

At this time, it's possible that Cameron Baird had never been drunk – abstinence born from his desire to become a professional footballer. Cam's reluctance to drink continued into infantry training, but Pete says he eventually buckled under the peer pressure.

Pete used to go to the bar, order as many pints as there were men, put a beer in front of Cam and gently chide him when he said he didn't want to drink it. 'I'm happy to drink your beer, Cam,' he would say, 'but by the time I get to it, it'll be warm.'

Cam relented, and eventually he developed a taste for icy-cold Victoria Bitter.

'Part of me thinks I shouldn't have done it,' Pete says, 'but it was the culture of the Army at that time and he ended up having a ball on those weekends.'

Cam and Pete would talk over a drink about the lives they'd been living before joining the Army. Cam would happily chat about his parents and his brother, but not about football. He wanted to be considered a soldier now, not some ex–footy player. His life was to be defined by this new goal. One boozy night, however, Cam started talking to Pete about why he'd joined up. His emotion when talking about football explained why he hadn't just tried to get drafted the next year, or nominated for the rookie draft.

'He was very angry at footy, and at the AFL. He felt like he'd been sold a lie, in a way,' says Pete. 'I'd watch him at infantry school, and I don't think he was ever destined to be an AFL player. That bloke was a soldier, through and through.'

A number of men who went through infantry training with Cam describe their difficulty in keeping up with someone who had the fitness of a professional athlete. But Cameron's excellence as a soldier wasn't just physical; he also had the right mental attitude, an aptitude for 'controlled aggression'.

Almost uniquely in the Australian workforce, an infantry soldier must have a willingness, an ability and even a desire to kill. Many courses within infantry training therefore require the simulated 'killing' of human-like targets. In those tasks, Cameron Baird excelled, his bayonet skills particularly ferocious.

In a letter to Doug and Kaye while at Singleton, Cam said his trainers were 'extremely happy with my aggression'. However, there were still hints of the civilian boy he'd so recently been. Cam wrote how much he loved and missed his parents, and said he didn't realise how much he had until he'd gone to Kapooka.

—

Near the end of their infantry training, soldiers nominate the unit they hope to join upon completion. Cam initially wanted to join the light infantry 1st Battalion, Royal Australian Regiment (or 1RAR). There were two reasons: first, 1RAR had a reputation as 'tough bastards', as Baird described them in a letter, and second, he believed it was the unit in which he would most quickly be deployed.

'As soon as you finish infantry training, you want to go to war as soon as possible, and Bairdy was no different,' says Pete Eisen. 'If anyone says they join the infantry because they like the exercise, they're full of shit.'

For Cam as an 18-year-old, SAS selection was pretty much out of the question for a number of years, but he fancied himself as a 1RAR sniper. He was attracted to the difficulty of the sniper's course, which required peak physical fitness and extreme concentration. He also thought the sniper's course was the toughest test the ADF could offer. This was incorrect, and Cameron would in time face a greater challenge.

One of the corporals running the infantry course suggested that Cam might like to apply for 4RAR, a unit that was slowly transforming from a regular infantry battalion into a special forces unit – specifically, a commando unit. Cameron said he barely knew what a commando did, but they trained hard, and that sounded good to him.

In the wake of the first Gulf War and operations in Somalia and the Balkans, it was believed that Western armies were less likely to engage in large-scale infantry battles in the coming years, and that they'd be more involved in cross-border raids and counter-insurgency operations. In the mid-1990s the decision was made that the ADF should increase its capacity for special-operations warfare.

The Army already had the SASR in Perth and the 1st Commando Regiment in Sydney. Both were well regarded, but the SASR was relatively small and had particular expertise in reconnaissance and infiltration, while the 1st Commando Regiment was a reserve unit. It was decided that a new, larger special forces regiment should be raised.

In 1997, therefore, the 4th Battalion of the Royal Australian Regiment was rebranded as 4RAR, and the unit started retraining those infantrymen who wanted to work towards a Sherwood green beret, the distinct headdress of a commando since 1941.

The modern use of *commando* arose during World War II, but the term's origins stretch back to the Boer War. In that conflict, some irregular Dutch fighters eschewed modern military techniques of the day, instead employing the hunting and field skills they had spent years learning. These fast-moving, mounted Boer infantry units called themselves *kommando*, and proved very effective against the British troops, who, dressed in their red coats and shiny buttons, were still trained to attack by lining up and walking slowly towards the enemy. When the raiders gained a reputation in the British press, they were often referred to as *commandos*. The name stuck.

When World War II broke out, British military planners suggested the term *commando* for their new specialised raiding units, which would later become the Special Air Service. The idea was that they would have the same marksmanship and hit-and-run efficacy of the Boer raiders.

When elevating 4RAR to a commando unit, it was decided that the unit's insignia should be the Fairbairn-Sykes dagger, used by British commandos in World War II. It was set against a double diamond background, a nod to the patches that Australian commandos wore in the same conflict.

The sandy beret of the SASR had long demanded respect in the Australian military, and the hope was that the green beret of the Australian commando would one day do the same. Like the SASR beret, a commando's green beret meant not just that he was a member of the unit, but also that he was fully qualified to be part of the reinforcement cycle.

Soldiers already in 4RAR were encouraged either to undertake special forces selection or to transfer to another infantry unit, and a distinction soon developed between those who were 'beret-qualified' and those who were not.

By the time Cameron Baird marched out of Singleton, two commando companies had been raised within 4RAR – Charlie and Bravo – but not all their men were beret-qualified. It was an incomplete unit, still searching for personality and purpose.

When Cam moved into the 4RAR 'lines', or housing, at Sydney's Holsworthy Barracks, he did so with a large group of new recruits who'd shown the requisite aptitude and aggression in their infantry training. He was living on the Tobruk Lines, Spartan accommodations built in the 1960s to house men who were on their way to the Vietnam War. The boys called their accommodation 'Hotel Hell', dubbing the nearby soldiers' boozer 'The Spew Club'. To say that life on the lines for the many young potential warfighters was full and rambunctious would be an understatement.

When not training, the lines were like a frat house on Red Bull. Booze was drunk, card games were played, windows were smashed – including one by Cam, who covered up the crime with a large AC/DC poster. Some nights the soldiers headed out to hit the nearby boozers, looking for girlfriends, but Cam didn't join them. He explained to his parents in letters that he was forsaking that pursuit and instead saving his money so he could buy an aquarium and some exotic fish. What he was actually doing was saving for a motorbike.

With deployment to East Timor almost a certainty – the unit would be used there as a regular infantry battalion – the men had to prepare. As well, many young recruits, including Cam, undertook a Commando Basic Training Course back at Singleton, a first step towards beret qualification.

Normally a glutton for punishment, Cam describes being underfed, under-slept and overtrained on the gruelling course, which was conducted by men from 1 Commando and the SASR. 'Fucking hell, no one said the Army was going to be this hard,' he wrote to his parents.

One of the instructors was Hans Fleer, a grizzled and intimidating Vietnam veteran who had received a Distinguished Conduct Medal (bar only the Victoria Cross, the highest commendation in the Australian military) after nine of his colleagues were hit by a Viet Cong machine gun and he pulled them to safety while under fire.

Fleer was known as Major Fleer but had an honorary rank of colonel, and it was common knowledge he'd been one of the original 'phantoms of the jungle', a moniker the Viet Cong gave to the SASR.

Fleer ran the young men ragged, constantly testing them physically and emotionally. At the start of the course, they were given a huge information pack, on the last page of which was a sheet about the specific role of the commando on the battlefield. One evening, after a full day of exhausting training, the soldiers were taken to a nearby hay shed, where plastic desks and chairs had been set up. The exhausted men sat down and Major Fleer drilled them on theory. Many stuttered their way through what they could remember.

Then Major Fleer called on one of the soldiers who'd excelled in the course for an answer. 'Private Baird, can you please tell me what the role of the commando is?'

There was a pregnant pause as the men tried to remember the last page of their information pack.

'To kill cunts?' Baird replied.

There was laughter from the men, but only after Fleer had allowed himself a smile.

'Perhaps not a complete answer, Private Baird, but that is a component of the job.'

Even though it was often disguised as something else, creating an unwavering ability to kill was a large part of that initial commando training. So, too, the ability to comfortably be exposed to enemy fire and the threat of death, and continue at the job at hand.

Back at the Tobruk Lines Cam would often sit out the front of his dormitory, playing guitar and welcoming all and sundry in for a chat. One day a neighbour on the lines, Eddie Robertson, sat down and introduced himself.

Like Cam, Eddie, who had grown up in Albury, on the border between New South Wales and Victoria, had joined the military straight out of school. Both of his grandfathers had served in World War II, but it was an uncle, who had served in 2RAR during the Vietnam War, who spurred him on to join the Army.

'He talked about the camaraderie,' Eddie said of his uncle's stories. 'He said you could be in a foxhole with someone and you might not have had much to do with him yet – you might not even know his name – but you'd share a brew and a razor and all of a sudden you'd do anything for him.'

It was in Cameron Baird that Eddie would find the camaraderie he was looking for. Cam would become one of his best mates, and someone he would share some intense combat situations with.

An easy fellow to speak to, with a strong sense of humour and a ready smile, Eddie Robertson became one of Cam's favourite blokes to work with, not just because he was personable, but because he was as dedicated to the art of soldiering and fighting as Cam.

Eddie recalls very fondly those early days on the lines with Cam, training, drinking, chatting and watching (and rewatching) the DVDs that circulated around the base. Nineties sex comedies and war and martial arts films were usually the most popular among the young soldiers, but the clear favourite at Holsworthy that year was the 1999 David Fincher cult classic *Fight Club*.

Containing themes of anti-consumerism and independent thought, the film also speaks about a lost masculinity that can be regained by engaging in a 'fight club', where friends closer than brothers beat the shit out of each other and learn something along the way. Of course, it didn't take long for the young commandos-in-waiting to start their own fight club, in a room above the vinyl-floored boozer close to their lines.

Two pairs of sixteen-ounce gloves were procured, and a schedule of fights between willing participants composed. The rules were never explicit, but a certain type of fighting – biting, or strikes to the groin – was discouraged. When a combatant no longer wanted to fight, or if the sense had been knocked out of him, then the contest would be over.

For a period, the fight club met every night. The beers would flow, the punches would fly, the blood would drip, but at the end of the night all was as it should be. The combatants might be sporting some cuts and bruises, but these weren't noticed amid the knocks they were picking up in their daily training.

One night Cam signed up for a fight. The soldiers organising the schedule arranged for him to fight a bloke named Adam, who was tall and fit but who hadn't filled out yet. As the men waited for Cam, Eddie says it was like something from *Mad Max Beyond Thunderdome*, another film that was popular on the base.

A bloodthirsty chant went up – 'Bairdy! Bairdy! Bairdy! Bairdy!' – and Cam's opponent, who had never met him before, looked around with some trepidation. Cam was downstairs, watching TV, and when he heard his name he took off his shirt and walked into the room, arms aloft and with a big grin on his face, enjoying the theatre.

'He wasn't a pugilist, more of a thrasher,' Eddie remembers with a laugh. 'Even though his technique was awful, he got in some good shots, and when Adam had sprawled out on the floor with a black eye and a busted nose, the grin came back and Cam checked if he was all right.

'That showed what kind of soldiers they were making us into. You couldn't do this job unless you had violence in you, but they wanted for us to be able to control that violence. Turn it on and off.'

Pete Eisen echoes those sentiments: 'As a commando, they're training us to have aggression, but to bottle it up, bottle it up, bottle it up – and then let it all go when it's the right time.'

A few days later, one of the fight club participants got a perforated eardrum and required medical assistance.

Adhering to the first rule of fight club, the soldier gave a less than truthful answer about how he'd sustained his injury. The non-commissioned officers started an informal investigation into what their increasingly battered and bruised young recruits were doing at night.

One day the company sergeant major (CSM), an old-school paratrooper in his forties, assembled the young soldiers on the parade ground. He was wearing his Sherwood green beret, unusual for an informal gathering, and proceeded to give them a light bollocking.

'Gentlemen, I hear there's an organisation that has been established going by the name of "fight club". Well, I want to tell you about another organisation we have: "pack club". We meet every Friday after knock-off, and we go on really, really long walks in the bush, wearing very, very heavy packs on our back. They're complementary organisations, actually.'

The boys saw the warning for what it was. It was a reprimand because there had to be one, but it was a friendly, perhaps even encouraging one from a senior NCO.

This commando unit was not envisioned as a mirror of that other special forces unit over in Perth – it was meant to be something else. The SASR might conduct direct action operations, but its soul was patience and stealth. The soul of the commando unit was violence and aggression. Always it had to be tempered and controlled, but it must exist in every man who donned the green beret. The trainers knew this and fostered a culture that enabled it. While a 'fight club' couldn't possibly be endorsed in any Australian workplace, in 4RAR it wasn't the scandal it might have been elsewhere.

There were a few other incidents that were also written off as acceptable masculine misadventure, like the time Bairdy lost his two front teeth.

Cam and Eddie were training on the Remington 870 shotgun Masterkey, a door-breaching weapon with a folding stock and one hell of a kick. The instructor informed the men that the weapon always required two hands, with the stock nestled in the operator's armpit.

Cameron disagreed. 'Reckon I can shoot this thing with one hand?' he asked Eddie.

Eddie nodded. He didn't know whether it was possible, but he wouldn't mind seeing his giant mate have a go.

Boom! The butt of the weapon leapt backwards and into Cam's mouth, breaking his two front teeth. Blood was pouring out, but Eddie and Cam collapsed laughing.

There was also the time that Cam finally got that motorbike he'd been saving for. He had a military motor-cycle licence, but had never bothered getting the civilian licence transfer he needed in order to ride it on New South

Wales roads. However, that didn't stop him from using it as his primary mode of transport when he was off the base.

One day, while riding across the Sydney Harbour Bridge, Cam clipped a divider, lost control of the bike and went over the top of the handlebars. The bike was wrecked, and so too was one of Cam's arms, but his primary concern at the time was whether the accident would have any legal consequences, and how this might affect his standing in the military.

Not wanting any of his new Army friends to know about the fall, Cam rang Brendan and said he was going to need help moving the wrecked bike. Brendan was happy to help, but he was in Albury, a six-hour drive away.

With adrenaline in his veins and no one there to help him, Cam got the bike upright and, steering with his good arm, muscled it along one of Sydney's busiest thoroughfares, onto the Kirribilli off-ramp and into a parking spot, miraculously without seeing any police. He got the bike sorted and later went to the Army infirmary, telling a fanciful story about falling from a friend's bike. His arm was broken.

Eddie laughs as he remembers the figure of misadventure that his mate looked at the time. 'With his arm in a cast and a perfect semi-circle gap in his teeth, he looked like a bit of a mess.'

Cam continued training, though, with a pace and passion that Eddie and Pete say was rarely matched by any other soldier. Roping, demolition, close-quarters battle, parachuting, range shooting, heavy weapons targeting – Cameron Baird threw himself into all of it, body and soul.

—

Midway through 2000, the young soldiers were sent on their first operation. It wouldn't be a plane trip away, but a mere bus ride.

Since the Munich Olympic Games in 1972, when 11 Israeli athletes and officials and a West German policeman were killed by Palestinian militants, Olympic Organising Committees have had strong counter-terrorism contingency plans in place. The Sydney Organising Committee decided that its counter-terrorism requirements for the 2000 Games went beyond what the New South Wales Police Force could provide.

As part of what would be called 'Operation Gold', a group of SASR snipers and operators drilled for months at Olympic venues and Sydney landmarks, ready to respond to any terrorist incidents. They were augmented by a contingent of Black Hawk helicopters, which could move the operators around the venues quickly. A group of 4RAR soldiers would augment the SASR; their brief was to create a cordon around any incident, as well as to serve as a general ready-response force.

4RAR's involvement in Operation Gold was part of a long-term plan the Army had to eventually establish a permanent counter-terrorism force on the east coast of Australia. Previously, Australia's only military counter-terrorism force was the Tactical Assault Group, raised from the SASR in Perth.

Another reason for including 4RAR in Operation Gold was to have 4RAR and SASR work together. Eventually, the two regiments would work as comparable units with complementary capabilities; they were not to be 'special forces' and 'special forces lite', although that was how many in the Army thought of it.

Dispelling that perception was going to take time. Many of the SASR operators were a lot older than the mostly teenaged 4RAR soldiers like Cam, Eddie and Pete, young men who had never been deployed and had only a fraction of the training of the blokes from Perth. There had also been a short period in which those who had made it through the last two weeks of SASR selection but subsequently failed the course were invited to join 4RAR; that did nothing for the prestige of the Sydney-based unit.

For 4RAR, Operation Gold turned out being a lot of sitting around. At the end of it, most of the blokes were keen to get back to Holsworthy, with an eye on gaining beret qualification and taking part in the first deployment of their military lives – to the world's newest country.

CHAPTER FOUR

A SINGULAR FOCUS

*'She was very striking, but maybe
not what I was expecting.'*

DOUG BAIRD

AIDABALATEN, EAST TIMOR
HOLSWORTHY, NEW SOUTH WALES
2001–02

Portugal's spice traders first ventured to the Timorese land-
mass in the 1500s. From that time until the Carnation
Revolution in Lisbon in 1974, the European power had,
in one way or another, governed the area we now know
as East Timor.

When Portugal's first democratic, anti-colonial government was installed after the revolution, East Timor had

a real chance at statehood. In 1975 a group called the Revolutionary Front for an Independent East Timor (known as Fretilin) declared East Timor an independent state and for eight days hope grew for the region's people. Then, on the ninth day, Indonesia invaded the nascent state and declared it its 27th province.

Although the United Nations refused to acknowledge Indonesia's claims to the territory, Australia, Great Britain and the United States accepted the invasion. Australia even accepted mineral concessions that, to many, looked a lot like a bribe.

For more than 20 years, a low-level war between Fretilin and the Indonesian military simmered. The East Timorese were brutalised, starved and even massacred by the Indonesian military and pro-Indonesian militias. Amnesty International estimates that some 200 000 people, a third of East Timor's population, died due to the Indonesian occupation.

International interest in the plight of the East Timorese people ebbed and flowed until 1999, after a governmental upheaval in Jakarta, the new Indonesian president, B.J. Habibie, announced a referendum on East Timorese state-hood. He claimed it would not only show that Indonesia was reforming, but would also likely provide an economic net positive. Despite bullying and beatings from the

pro-Indonesian militias, turnout at the August 1999 referendum was high, and more than 75 per cent of the East
Timorese people voted for independence.

This result unleashed a violent response from the
militias, which included large-scale massacres and mass
relocations. International pressure on Indonesia grew as
scenes of murder and looting started to reach Western
TV screens. Soon the United Nations and Australia were
calling for a peacekeeping force to be sent to the region.

President Habibie was under external pressure to
allow an intervention, but Indonesia's senior military –
especially those from Kopassus, the Indonesian special
forces – resisted. There's no doubt that at least some of
the Indonesian colonels and generals were working with the
militias in their campaign of terror and slaughter; perhaps
they feared war crimes charges in the aftermath of an
international intervention.

In September 1999 a United Nations force, named the
International Force for East Timor (or INTERFET) and
led by Australia, under the command of Major-General
Peter Cosgrove, was deployed to East Timor. Even with
President Habibie's approval, however, it wasn't known
how Indonesia's military and the militias they sponsored
would respond to what they might interpret as an invasion.

An international special forces group called Response Force, made up mostly of SASR operators but with some British Special Boat Service and New Zealand SAS soldiers, was one of the first units in East Timor. After securing the airport, they conducted reconnaissance missions, looking for lurking militiamen, as well as Kopassus soldiers who had reportedly been coordinating with the militia.

A few weeks into the relatively peaceful interdiction, an intelligence report was filed that suggested a large number of armed militiamen were massing in a village close to the Indonesian border. A six-man SASR patrol was sent out on a reconnaissance mission to verify the report. If it was correct, an entire squadron of SASR soldiers would be sent to confront the enemy.

The Black Hawk helicopter that inserted the team was detected by the militia, and patrols were sent out to find the Australians. When one of the militia patrols intercepted the SASR team, a firefight ensued in which between four and six militia members were killed. The SASR sustained no casualties.

INTERFET operated in East Timor until February 2000, when it handed over peacekeeping duties to a 23-country UN Peacekeeping Force led, again, by Australia.

In April 2001 Cam Baird and 4RAR were deployed to East Timor, landing in Dili before being loaded up in

Unimog trucks for the journey up to Aidabalaten, not far from where the SASR firefight had happened. This battalion-sized deployment would be the last time 4RAR would go into a warzone with a mix of beret-qualified and unqualified soldiers. As such, they were used only as regular infantry.

The trip from the airbase in Darwin to Dili lasted only a couple of hours, and it wasn't expected that the soldiers would see any action, but the amped-up young men fresh out of grunt and commando training were ecstatic to be out of the country.

'Everyone was pretty excited to be over there, on deployment with loaded weapons,' says Eddie Robertson.

After relieving 1RAR, who had established a patrol base in an old school in Aidabalaten, 4RAR set up their planning cycle: every two weeks the four companies would rotate between duty at the patrol base; a stint at another patrol base nearby, designated 'Marko'; a 'green hat' patrolling phase, in which soldiers were sent out into the bush close to the border; and duty as the 'quick reaction force', to serve as reinforcements for any company that was in danger of being overwhelmed.

Cam said he literally dreamed of bumping into an armed Indonesian militia or Kopassus element while conducting a 'green hat' patrol, like the SASR operators had in 1999. The young commandos bristled with excitement when they patrolled closer to the Indonesian border, imagining themselves engaging with the bloodthirsty perpetrators of the massacres they'd heard about. But their fantasies would not be realised. Chopping up missionaries and terrified children with machetes is not the same thing as confronting fully armed Australian infantry battalions, so the militiamen were understandably not keen for any confrontation.

Mostly, 4RAR did the work of peacekeepers, setting up cordons and checkpoints, looking for signs of insurrection, showing a force presence to the locals and disrupting the crime that can often arise in times of political instability. There were very few contacts with the enemy while Cam was in East Timor. One, however, involved Cam's mate Pete Eisen, who was part of a patrol that confronted some armed Indonesians, and exchanged fire with them near the border.

It's likely the men the Australians confronted were just sandalwood thieves – and it's not known whether any of the Indonesians were hit – but for the young infantrymen, a contact was a contact.

'Cam was so fucking happy for me,' Pete says. 'He was jealous like the rest of them – we'd been working every moment of the last year towards getting in a gunfight – but he was happy for me. It was absolutely nothing compared to what those guys would see in Afghanistan, but it was something.'

In many ways, the most significant moment of Cam Baird's East Timor deployment had nothing to do with East Timor or Indonesia. It was shown on a small television inside their patrol base. One evening in Aidabalaten, a call went out to all the soldiers in the base not on the towers doing perimeter security to come immediately to the command post. This wasn't normal: something big must be happening.

When Eddie and Cam arrived, they found a group of soldiers already crowded around a small telly, which was showing the Manhattan skyline slowly filling with smoke. A passenger jet had crashed into the north tower of the World Trade Center. No one knew why or how, but fire was billowing out of the iconic building and there was already likely a significant loss of life. Then a second plane smashed into the south tower.

This was obviously no accident. In the silence, the young Australians tried to make sense of the event. None of them were foreign policy experts, but they knew what they were seeing would mean. 'We're going to war,' one of the soldiers said quietly.

He was right. They would be going to war, one with multiple fronts and multiple nations involved. The global 'War on Terror' continues to this day.

In the confusion of the days after the 9/11 attacks, the border with the Islamic nation of Indonesia was initially considered a potential flashpoint. 4RAR was placed on a state of heightened alert. As more information about the attacks came in, however, it was decided that 4RAR should return to Sydney so the men could extend their counter-terrorism capabilities.

In October 2001 a formal directive from the Australian cabinet instructed the Army to raise a Tactical Assault Group from 4RAR; it would be named TAG (East). While the SASR's TAG unit, now renamed TAG (West), would still respond to on-water incidents such as piracy or oil platform seizures, as well as international events involving Australians, TAG (East) would soon become responsible for most counter-terrorism operations on land in Australia. It would also be the first response unit for the east coast capitals.

When the infantrymen in 4RAR came back from East Timor, they found themselves in one of three designations. The first was soldiers who were beret-qualified or working towards beret qualification and who would take on a 'black role' within TAG (East). The second group contained soldiers who were beret-qualified or working towards beret qualification and would fulfil a warfighting or 'green role'. The third category was for soldiers who weren't planning to become beret-qualified; they would ultimately be shifted to other units.

In the wake of 9/11, many of the most promising young soldiers in 4RAR, including Cam Baird, were invited to undertake a 'black role', which would be handled by Charlie Company. Cam wasn't interested. Although counter-terrorism work would be something he'd enthusiastically embrace later, when all four commando companies rotated in and out of TAG (East), for the time being he wanted to get his beret and become a 'green role' expert.

This was a period of extreme concentration and dedication for Cameron Baird. He started ticking off commando courses like a diligent boy scout, and the most difficult and arduous tasks became his favourites. From low-opening parachute jumps to intense pack marches, Baird only wanted to train, regardless of what that training was. He even enjoyed 'parachute load follow' training, in which the soldiers were tossed out of a plane over the sea with all the components required for a beach insertion.

This was a task other soldiers describe as nothing but hard. 'You get chucked out [of the plane] and you'd all be spread over a mile,' says Eddie, 'with the boats and engines and spilled fuel in the choppy ocean making you nauseous. You'd have to get out of your parachute and into your fins, and it was a nightmare. Cam loved it, though – anything that was challenging. He liked to test himself; he was just one of those guys.'

'After East Timor he seemed to become a different bloke,' says Rick Green, Cam's high-school friend from Gladstone Park who would send guitar and girlie magazines to Cam when he was on deployment. 'He just seemed to be so serious and focused, which we certainly weren't.'

The commandos were training for a war which they knew was only a phone call away. It had become apparent that the first shots of the War on Terror would be fired in the central Asian nation of Afghanistan. Australia is the only country that has fought in every war the United States has been in since World War II, and so it was expected that Australia would contribute militarily to the US invasion of Afghanistan, but the question remained: would 4RAR be part of the commitment?

'In the lead-up to Afghanistan we all had a collective understanding that things were going to change,' Eddie says, 'but we didn't know if we were going to get a run there. They were sending an SAS troop over there, but as more info came in about Afghan and the Yanks and the Taliban came up, we wondered if it was just going to blow over. We all wanted to be ready, though.'

When the invasion started, the men of 4RAR watched it on television with a sense of disappointment. The Taliban were being monumentally routed; none of the Aussies thought the conflict would last longer than a couple of weeks. Their hope was that American vengeance over the attacks on New York and the Pentagon would not end with Afghanistan. When the next war started, they wanted to be ready for it.

There was little fanfare when Cam was awarded his commando beret in 2002. These days there's a ceremony, but Cam got nothing more than a handshake from an NCO. After becoming beret-qualified, he moved into the reinforcement or 'reo' cycle, where he ended up at Bravo Company, a place he would come to consider home.

—

Cam and Eddie trained hard during the week at Holsworthy, but on weekends they enjoyed the nightlife – such as it is – of the nearby Sydney suburb of Liverpool. A staunchly working-class area, Liverpool was not particularly cosmo-politan, but it had Chinese restaurants, working-men's clubs and bars, all of which served Victoria Bitter. It was all they needed.

A favourite nocturnal activity of Cam's in that period was karaoke, which was offered at an Irish bar called Flynn's, and on Fridays at a local Chinese restaurant. With a belly full of Mongolian lamb and VB, Cam loved to warble his way through classic rock staples. (Cam's voice was once described to me as 'powerful', and many times as 'awful'.) It was on one of these nights out that he met Robin.

Robin would become a very important part of Cam's life, but she has chosen not to be involved in this book. With respect for her wish for privacy, details of her life, except those that are essentially pertinent in telling Cam's story, will not be revealed.

It's not known whether Cam approached Robin or she him, but Eddie says Cam had a propensity for approaching people at bars, keen to learn the details of their life, so it's easy to imagine that he approached her.

Looking back, it seems Cam was attracted to a particular type of woman: blondes with long, straight hair and a commanding way about them. He had a soft spot for the Australian actress Rebecca Gibney and the American singer Anastacia, and told his mates he saw elements of both of them in Robin. Cam also told friends that his initial attraction to Robin was the ease with which he could speak to the attractive protective services officer.

A romance was beckoning, but for one thing: there was a sizeable age difference. When Cam met Robin he was 20 years old. Robin was more than a decade older than him. Initially, both Cam and Robin were concerned about this. When they met, Cam had assumed the striking blonde was younger than she actually was. Robin thought the opposite about Cam.

To ease any tension about this, the pair established early in their relationship a rule that would extend throughout: either could leave the relationship at any time, for any reason, without any argument or consternation. This was a sworn promise, and Cam was especially strict about keeping a promise.

Robin and Cam started spending most of their spare time together, with Cam regularly staying at Robin's house nearby, or Robin staying with Cam on the lines. To some, it was strange to see the impeccably dressed and mature Robin sneaking in and out of the soldiers' accommodation, but she seemed happy to bear the mild ignominy to spend time with her man.

As the relationship progressed, Cam, the son of two self-confessed traditionalists, decided that he should introduce his girlfriend to his parents. He called Kaye and told her he'd met someone in Sydney. His mother was happy for him. He said she was a bit older than him. Kaye said that was fine, as long as she wasn't, like, thirty. Cam stayed silent.

Shortly after that conversation, Cam flew down to Melbourne to visit his parents. What they didn't know was that he'd brought Robin with him. On his first night at home, after dinner, Cam told his mum and dad that Robin was in town, and that he hoped that they could all catch up the next day. Doug and Kaye were eager to meet the woman their younger son was seeing.

The next morning, Doug and Cam drove into the centre of Melbourne to pick Robin up from the hotel where she was staying. Doug vividly remembers seeing Robin for the first time: she was standing waiting for them wearing leather boots, leather pants and a leather top.

Doug introduced himself and Robin got into the car. Doug and Cam sat in the front seats, and Robin was in the back. As they drove to the family home, Doug kept sneaking glances at Robin in the rear-view mirror. 'She was very striking,' he says, 'but maybe not what I was expecting. You could say it was awkward, to say the least.'

Over lunch, Doug and Kaye started to build a rapport with Robin. Their only concern was their son's contentment, and he seemed to care deeply about her – and she him.

'I was really happy because they just clicked, you know?' says Doug. 'I've got photos of them later with his hand on her leg, on the couch – you know, that nice stuff.'

Soon Cam and Robin moved into defence housing together, but, unlike many couples within the unit, the Army didn't define their social lives. Robin was always friendly with the men in Cam's unit and their significant others, but she was reluctant to become too close.

When a company goes away on a combat deployment, the wives and girlfriends, and the men from the other units, rally together, and provide each other with great support against the loneliness and tension of being left behind. Robin had little interest in this aspect of Army life.

When Cam left Sydney for his first major deployment, one of Robin's main pillars of support would be his mother, Kaye. She would spend many hours on the phone with Robin, making small talk and trying to avoid conversations about chemical weapons and such things. He may have been a long way from home, but Cameron made sure Robin knew he cared for her by arranging with a local florist to make regular deliveries to her while he was away.

That deployment took place in February 2003, and was very different from the relatively more benign mission to protect the East Timorese from sandalwood thieves and militiamen. 4RAR was going to Iraq, where a real war beckoned. The only question was how deeply Cam and his fellow commandos would get into the action.

CHAPTER FIVE

BAGHDAD DASH

'Fuck, I wish I'd been up there on the gun.'

CAMERON BAIRD

IRAQ
2003

Saddam Hussein had been in the sights of US President George W. Bush and a group of American neoconservative politicians and diplomats for many years before the 2003 invasion. The United States' relationship with Iraq had been acrimonious for decades. Hussein wasn't only a vicious dictator, disrespectful of the sovereignty of his neighbours and with little regard for the human rights of his nation's citizenry, but he also threatened the energy security of the United States.

Although the two nations had momentarily aligned in the 1980s, when the United States gave battlefield intelligence and matériel support to the Iraqis while they fought the recently formed Islamic Republic of Iran, most of the modern history between the two countries was one of distrust, brinksmanship and, in the 1991 Gulf War, outright conflict.

Every US administration since President Carter's had its proponents of 'regime change' in Iraq, but never as many as in George W. Bush's, nor in such positions of power. A self-defined interventionist, the second President Bush believed in spreading American values across the world, and most senior officials in both the Department of Defense and the State Department shared that view.

Shortly after coming into office in early 2001, the Republican president had officials at State and Defense working on contingency plans for an invasion of Iraq, should a *casus belli* emerge. Then one did.

On 11 September 2001, fifteen Saudi Arabian men, two men from the United Arab Emirates, one man from Lebanon and one man from Egypt hijacked four commercial jets. Two smashed into New York's World Trade Center, one hit the Pentagon, in Washington DC, and in the other plane the hijacking was thwarted by the passengers, and it crashed in a field in Pennsylvania. Two days later President

Bush called for the invasion plans, ready to respond to the 9/11 attacks by declaring war with Iraq.

Quickly it became apparent that Osama bin Laden and his al-Qaeda terrorist network were behind the 9/11 attacks, and that the United States would first have to hit bin Laden's hosts and sponsors, the Taliban, rulers of Afghanistan.

Even as the first bombs dropped on Kabul, however, the Bush Administration's plans to topple Saddam progressed. Whether Iraq was involved in the 9/11 attacks or not, the neocons had decided that the removal of Hussein and his Ba'ath Party was now of paramount importance.

In November 2001, with the Afghan war only a month old, US Secretary of Defense Donald Rumsfeld ordered the commander of the United States Central Command (or CENTCOM), General Tommy Franks, to prepare for a 'decapitation' of the Iraqi leadership. In 2002 a joint resolution of US Congress authorised military action against Iraq, should President Bush deem it necessary. In 2003 the case for war was argued to the United Nations.

The congressional resolution had cited humanitarian concerns and Iraq's aspirations for regional expansion as justification for military action, but the primary argument being made to the rest of the world was that Saddam Hussein was reconstituting his weapons of mass destruction

(WMD) program, and that his government had a secret relationship with al-Qaeda, which created the possibility of the terrorist entity gaining access to nuclear, chemical or biological weapons.

After the congressional resolution passed, the US government claimed a right to unilaterally attack Iraq, but nevertheless it sought the support of other nations – for both strategic and visibility purposes. Few nations would agree to act against a sovereign state without a United Nations resolution supporting the proposal, but Australia's prime minister, John Howard, quickly assured the Americans that Australia would stand with the United States, no matter what.

The Australian public were emphatically against the invasion of Iraq – an AC Nielsen poll found that only 6 per cent of the population agreed with military action in the absence of a UN resolution – but Howard was steadfast in his commitment to the Bush Administration and the war. 'We believe that it is very much in the national interest of Australia that Iraq have taken from her her chemical and biological weapons,' Prime Minister Howard told the National Press Club, 'and [be] denied the possibility of ever having nuclear weapons.'

Following 9/11, Howard had invoked the ANZUS Treaty of 1951, which meant Australia was obliged to offer military assistance should the United States be attacked. Now he claimed that an invasion of Iraq was part of the 'global War on Terror', which was a response to the attacks, and that Australia was not only morally bound to act against Iraq, but also treaty-bound.

There are many and varied opinions on the legality of the Iraq War and how it relates to Australia's obligations under the ANZUS Treaty, but most agree that Howard's claim would have been much stronger if the United Nations had authorised the invasion.

The legitimacy of a UN resolution was sought by the United States, with Bush even sending his well-respected and politically moderate secretary of state, Colin Powell, to address the Security Council. The evidence Powell presented could be described kindly as poorly vetted, and viciously as fabricated. We now know, however, that there was likely nothing the United Nations could have done to stop the United States and its partners from invading Iraq in 2003.

It has since been proven that Iraq had no undeclared stockpiles of WMDs, and it's highly unlikely that al-Qaeda ever had any relationship with Saddam Hussein or the Iraqi government. But that knowledge was years away, and the United States' hawkish leaders were poised to act immediately.

—

Ultimately, the Bush Administration decided to strike Iraq with the support of a 'Coalition of the Willing', which ended up constituting just the United Kingdom, Poland and Australia. A stocktake of these nations was made by US military planners, who took special interest in those units which best suited what would later become known as the 'Rumsfeld Doctrine'.

Secretary of State Rumsfeld was particularly interested in the capabilities of each country's special forces units, as he thought that, alongside recent communications and optics upgrades and fast cavalry, they could reshape the modern battlefield and be used to unprecedented effect. Ostensibly, Australia had two special forces assault elements. In the halls of power in both Canberra and Washington, there was great confidence in the mature and battle-tested SASR unit, but also questions as to whether the youthful 4RAR could yet be considered a full-bore special forces unit. They were commandos by name – but could they prove themselves worthy of that honour?

In planning Australia's commitment to the Iraq War, Howard was forced to tread a fine line between American acquiescence and the general Australian disapproval of the war. When hints were dropped that the United States might like Australia to deploy an element of ASLAVs – Australian Light Armoured Vehicles – to support the US 1st Marine Division in their charge towards Baghdad, Australia baulked; such a mission would almost certainly result in close combat for the Australians, and therefore also casualties. Howard knew that significant deaths or injuries in Iraq would create a political nightmare for him.

For their part, the commandos out at Holsworthy became increasingly excited about the possibility of deploying to Iraq. This was to be a war, a real one. Saddam Hussein had the fourth-largest standing army in the world. He also had three of the things the commandos had been training to destroy: tank divisions, encamped defensive positions and a large, elite Republican Guard, who would surely stand and fight.

'It wasn't that we were bloodthirsty or anything, it's just that we wanted to prove ourselves,' says Sam Bush, formerly of Bravo Company, and a good friend of Cam Baird's. 'We were a very young unit, and we really didn't want to miss out on the chance to get in and prove what we could do. We were like a footy team that had trained and trained and just wanted to get out there on the field and kick some goals.'

As decisions about their fate were made in Canberra, the men of 4RAR prepared for the kind of specialised warfighting that a commando unit could expect in Iraq. The unit was drilled more and more on offensive, direct-action operations, and their briefings became increasingly specific and more highly classified. There were briefings on Iraqi weapons systems, capabilities and troop numbers, while the tempo of drilling in chemical- and biological-resistant suits increased. Cam became expert in the use of heavy weapons such as the Javelin anti-tank missile.

In early 2003 a group of beret-qualified operators, including Cam, was told that in the coming months they might be subject to a surprise counter-terrorism interrogation – this was known as 'going in the bag'. It was a thrilling prospect for the guys, who saw in it an indication that their deployment to Iraq would soon be forthcoming.

This exercise is intended to simulate the experience of being captured on the battlefield by an antagonistic force. It is designed to gauge the operator's tolerance for the extreme conditions experienced in such an ordeal. In the briefing, Cam was told what should and should not be said to interrogators; he was told that he would likely become hallucinatory after over a day of interrogation.

A few weeks later, the men of Bravo Company were informed that they would be moving up to RAAF Amberley, in Queensland, for manoeuvres. As Cam and some of his Bravo Company mates made their way to the airbase, he wondered aloud whether this was going to be the moment they were going in the bag. Cam suggested that the guys go to Hungry Jack's and stuff themselves, just in case.

With bellies full of burgers and fries, the guys reported for duty – and were promptly snatched, gagged, blind-folded and taken to interrogation cells. Each man was kept awake and hungry, and was bombarded with questions – some of which they were allowed to answer, and others they could not. After seemingly endless hours of interrogation, the boys were released and allowed to go for a shower, a beer, a meal and a lie down.

A few weeks later, approximately 90 soldiers from Bravo – Cam among them – were told to start pre-deployment briefings. In April they made their way from Sydney to the Indian Ocean island of Diego Garcia; then it was on to the Middle East, where they waited for further orders.

Both 4RAR and the SASR were deployed to a then undisclosed Middle Eastern location. In early 2017 it was revealed in Fairfax newspapers that this was H5, or Prince Hassan Air Base, a Jordanian base about 70 miles (110 kilometres) north-east from the capital, Amman, which had previously been a pumping station on the old Mosul to Haifa oil pipeline.

The commandos and the SASR were ostensibly to be a partnered force, with complementary capabilities, but even before the war began there was tension between the two regiments, as the SASR did not yet see the commandos as their equals. This opinion was seemingly reflected on a command level also, with the Perth regiment given support that wasn't forthcoming to the commandos.

'When we first arrived there was no accommodation, then these dongas [prefab temporary accommodations] came so we moved in,' says Sam Bush. 'A few days later some Chinook pilots arrived, and they kicked us out. Straightaway we knew where we were in the pecking order. Every day it felt like we were looked at as the little kids on the block.'

Two days before the attempted 'decapitation strike' on 20 March 2003 – presumably the start of the war – the SASR flew, low and fast, into Iraq, with the American helicopters dropping them off in the dark desert. Although a squadron of Australian Chinooks had been stationed at H5, American MH-47D helicopters had been used to ferry the force; the Aussie Chinooks didn't have the electronic surface-to-air counter-measures that were needed to operate in Iraq.

The SASR mission was to find and destroy Scud missiles. This was a tactical, long-range ballistic missile that Saddam Hussein had been using since the Iran–Iraq War. The Scud was not the most accurate munition in the world, but could be fitted with biological or chemical warheads. As Saddam had proved in 1991, it could be flown at least as far as Israel.

Cam and the 4RAR boys were left at the base and told they would serve as a quick reaction force (QRF) for the SASR. But as the war started and American helicopter assets became scarce, the commandos would look at the Chinooks, which they knew were of little use on the battlefield, and wonder how they would get to the SASR, should they be needed.

Day after day, Cam and the Bravo boys were ready at H5, and every day would end without them getting the call they so desperately wanted. They'd get snippets of news about the war, the bombing campaign, the push to Baghdad and the actions of the Australians. The SASR had been in a series of gunfights, but – unfortunately for Cam – none of the fights amounted to anything the Perth boys could not handle.

It has since been noted that, if the commandos were to be an effective QRF, they probably should have been stationed somewhere within Iraq. Many wonder whether they would ever have been trusted with QRF duties, should one of the SASR battles have got out of control.

Another stated role of 4RAR was combat search and rescue (CSAR), meaning if coalition planes (including

Australian F/A-18 Hornet fighter jets, which had been in operation) were to go down in western Iraq, the 4RAR would have been tasked with securing the site and extracting the pilots. Based in Jordan, however, with the Chinooks unable to enter Iraq, it seems unlikely that they would ever have been called into action, even if a pilot in their area of operations (AO) had gone down and needed rescue.

Either way, the Iraqi air force was in no position to fight the coalition in the air; nor were Iraq air defence capabilities able to threaten coalition pilots and planners. In fact, Iraqi resistance was, in the air and on the land, far more insipid and less organised than the US military planners had assumed.

On 16 April the SASR rolled into one of Iraq's largest military installations, the Al Asad Airbase, which sits about 100 kilometres north-west of Ramadi, in the so-called Sunni Triangle. They found it all but undefended. A small number of Iraqi four-wheel drives, mortars and machine guns were deployed against the SASR, but with air support the enemy force was overwhelmed very quickly.

After accepting defeat from the Iraqi forces and securing detainees, the relatively small SASR element commandeered two bulldozers, a grader and a roller, and used them to fill in the bomb holes in one of the airfield's runways. When they were finished, the commandos were finally called in.

A week after Baghdad had fallen, Cameron and the other 4RAR soldiers were loaded into a C-130 Hercules, and finally touched down in the Iraq War. As he would do for all of his four deployments in Afghanistan, Cam Baird hit the ground first and hit it hard.

Before the C-130 Hercules even landed, Cam was vibrating out of his seat. As the plane came to a halt and the load doors started to open – first the top door and then the bottom ramp – he leapt out onto the runway. With his pack, rifle and ammo, Baird was laden and landed heavily, jarring his body, and likely damaging a disc in his lower back. The pain would have been significant, but Cam showed no indication of it – on that day or on any other during the deployment. It would, however, prove to be a debilitating injury.

—

Baird's wasn't the only back injury a commando suffered on that trip. Almost every man on that deployment spoke to me of carrying far more weight than he should have, having loaded himself up with ammunition, food and water. They all felt as though they would be in the desert for weeks, not just the few days they'd need before being resupplied. This was in stark contrast to the stripped-down kit the commandos bore when getting on helicopters for their last tours of Afghanistan, when they had to be ready for gunfights that involved sprinting, jumping and sometimes even hand-to-hand combat.

At Al Asad Cam saw the power of the coalition bombing, and also how unprepared the Iraqis had been for war. Amid bomb craters and destroyed buildings at the base, more than 50 Soviet-era MIGs and other combat planes were discovered, but many were unserviceable. Some had been pushed off runways and into date groves when the bombing campaign had begun; others had been destroyed. (In time some would go back into the air as part of a new Iraqi air force.)

Nearly 8 million kilograms of ordnance was found and secured at the base, which was an important haul as Al Asad was relatively close to the population centres that would become known as the 'triangle of death' when the Iraqi insurgency started.

Bravo Company stayed on the airbase for two weeks in preparation for the arrival of an American cavalry regiment, which was to take control of it. Afterwards, they were flown back to Jordan. A few days after the majority of 4RAR left the country, President Bush flew onto the USS *Abraham Lincoln*, which had just returned from operations in the Persian Gulf, and declared that 'major combat operations have ended'.

Fourteen years after that speech, the men of Bravo are still being deployed to Mosul to help in the fight against the insurgents who emerged in 2003. At the time, however, the war for most of the commandos was over. Only two teams of six men – including Cam Baird and Sam Bush – remained, for a job in the increasingly violent capital of Baghdad.

After President Bush's now derided 'mission accomplished' speech, there was pressure in Washington and Canberra for Australia to establish a diplomatic presence in Baghdad as quickly as possible. It was thought to be important to bring a sense of normalcy to the city, and the Australian government wanted to be able to gather intelligence first-hand in the newly seized capital.

An element of SASR troopers, augmented by a small group of spooks and intrepid diplomats, would be the eyes and ears of Canberra, backed up by an infantry element – Bairdy and the boys. This group would be called the Baghdad Security Group (BSG).

—

One of the first missions of the BSG was to find and establish a site for the new Australian embassy. Camping at the old embassy, the commandos spent the early days of the mission touring the recently conquered city, looking for a site that could be defended, and one relatively close to the International Zone (which was also known as the Green Zone).

An appropriate site was found in the neighbourhood of Babil, a couple of kilometres south of the Green Zone and sitting in a fold of the Tigris River. The commandos established a barracks next to the embassy in a large, heart-shaped building, which was in very good nick, bar one large hole that had been made by a tank round. They set up security protocols and prepared to be at the beck and call of the diplomats and spooks.

Sam Bush remembers Baghdad as relatively quiet in those early days, with people going about their business and waiting for whatever was coming next. The site of the old embassy was a predominantly Christian neighbourhood, and Sam says the people there seemed particularly thankful that Saddam was gone. He remembers an old man who lived across the road from their building, and who made a point of bringing strong, sugary tea to the Australian soldiers whenever he saw them. But as the days passed, Sam says, there was more and more talk of a city that was simmering with tension, ready to boil over.

'A lot of the people started talking about the "Baghdad dash",' he recalls. 'Coalition forces had tried to get to Baghdad so quickly that there were concerns that none of the ground behind them had really been secured, and some of the guys we met were of the opinion that it was all going to go to shit pretty soon.'

On 21 April the Coalitional Provisional Authority (CPA), a transitional government entity with complete executive, legislative and judicial control over Iraq, was established. On 16 May 'Coalitional Provisional Authority Order Number One' was issued, which stated that members of the previously ruling Ba'ath Party be 'removed from their positions and banned from future employment in the public sector'. This meant that almost all Iraqi police and army personnel were instantly out of work, as were a great number of civil servants in a highly bureaucratised city. In the Iraqi education ministry alone, more than 16 000 people were dismissed, with no chance of re-employment. Instantly Baghdad was a city awash with disgruntled men, many broke, armed and with at least some military experience. After the order, Sam often heard gunfire echoing through the city, reminding him how little order had actually been established.

Then, one day in Baghdad, Cam and his commando element finally got their first taste of combat. It would only be a morsel, but they hungrily devoured it anyway.

A member of the diplomatic mission wanted to meet with an Iraqi contact, so it was arranged that the pair would convene at a nearby restaurant. A security detail was raised for the trip, with each BSG team manning a Mitsubishi Triton truck outfitted with MAG 58 general support machine guns. The two trucks were to 'top and tail' the diplomatic vehicle, which was bulletproof, reinforced and had a number of SASR operators inside.

After parking, the commandos set themselves up outside the restaurant, with their machine guns in view of a street which was largely unlit and relatively quiet. An hour later they were on the road again. When they were nearly back at the Australian barracks, on a very dimly lit street, one of the guys in Cam's vehicle spotted a man holding what appeared to be a gun.

Before any call could be made on the radio, the man, who was indeed holding a machine gun, let off 10 to 15 rounds at the convoy. Sam Bush, in the turret of the Triton, let loose with his MAG 58 directly at the man and the convoy sped off to the embassy.

Back in the safety of the barracks (which was only relative, actually, as the site was attacked by car bombs in both 2004 and 2005), Cam had no end of questions for Sam. What was the bloke wearing? What was the weapon he used? How did he raise it? Did it look like he knew what he was doing? Were the rounds directed at the turret or the cab? Did you hit the bloke? *Did you hit the bloke?*

Bush wasn't sure. He had a bead on this guy, though, he said, so he reckoned he might have.

'Fuck, I wish I'd been up there on the gun,' Cam said.

He had given voice to the thoughts of every man in the BSG. They were one of the most highly trained forces in Australia, and here, at the end of a major war (or so they thought), most of them hadn't even loosened off a round.

Over the next couple of weeks there were two more incidents of random Iraqis taking pot shots at the soldiers or consular staff, but Cam was never on the gun when it was time to return fire; the commandos rotated between the gun, driver and passenger positions. Each incident was brief, and resolved quickly. After five weeks in Baghdad, Bravo was sent back to H5 and then, shortly after, to Sydney.

Sam Bush says the Middle Eastern deployments had the Bravo boys walking a little taller at Holsworthy than they had been when they left, but some of the lads, especially Cam, were abjectly disappointed. They considered that they'd been protected and mollycoddled – that they'd never really been there to fight. All the men felt confused by some of the decisions made by command.

For instance, on 13 April an element of commandos had been rushed to Baghdad airport to provide security for an RAAF Hercules carrying medical supplies and three Australian journalists into Baghdad. The mission was called

Operation Baghdad Assist, and it had been ordered after Baghdad hospitals were looted near bare.

The supplies were deposited on the tarmac and the feel-good stories were written, but the commandos went back to their barracks dissatisfied. They had not delivered the supplies to the hospitals because there was simply no safe way to get to them. The supplies rotted away next to the runway. Command had known this would be the case. The whole thing was nothing more than a photo op, but they ordered it to happen anyway. Australian special forces commander Lieutenant Colonel Rick Burr wrote in his diary that the operation 'made a mockery of our approach'.

In a 2003 classified document published by Fairfax papers in February 2017 after a freedom-of-information request, Dr Albert Palazzo from the Directorate of Army Analysis wrote of Operation Catalyst (as the Australian contribution to the invasion of Iraq was named) that the ADF was 'not ready for war' and 'struggled to articulate a mission for the troops it dispatched and maintained in the MEAO [Middle East Area of Operations]'.

Dr Palazzo specifically commented on how the 4RAR troops had been used: 'The commandos came to resent both the treatment they received from the SAS on a personal level and also the nature of the tasks they received on a professional one.' He noted that this had led to 'hostility and jealousy that soured the relationship'.

Tension between 2 Commando (as 4RAR is now known, after a name change in June 2009) and the SASR continues to this day, but it seems that Cam never had any time for it, and he never bore any animosity towards the Perth-based men. However, his Iraq experiences did seriously sour his relationship with command.

When Cam returned home he was awarded, along with some other minor medals, the Infantry Combat Badge. He told a fellow commando that he hadn't felt like he'd earned it. The Infantry Combat Badge was awarded to infantrymen who had spent 90 days or more in 'warlike operations', and Iraq qualified as 'warlike'. But Cam told his mates in the unit that the 4RAR Iraq tour was relatively trifling when compared to the kind of combat that other coalition soldiers, including the SASR, had experienced. Cam didn't believe he deserved the recognition.

He also felt that history was repeating itself. Once again he had trained to a standard of excellence that was acceptable to his own impossibly high requirements, and once again he'd not been given the opportunity to test his skills. In some ways, Iraq was to soldiering what the AFL draft had been to football.

To make matters worse, the back injury that he'd sustained when arriving in Iraq just would not go away. Cam tried to keep it secret from the other soldiers, and especially the bosses, but it was becoming obvious that there were some tasks that the usually physically dominant Baird could no longer do. Some weeks, when the pain in his back was extreme, his duties on base were limited to serving drinks at the boozer.

He feared things might get worse, and that he would be stuck in military limbo, unable to do the courses required if he was to stay in the reinforcement cycle. Then what would he do? Cam was no barracks soldier.

On a trip back home to Gladstone Park, Cam visited a chiropractor, and was told that his back could probably be rehabilitated but he'd have to take it easy for an extended period of time – perhaps months, possibly even a year.

Dissatisfied with his experiences in Iraq and unsettled by his injury, Cam started to wonder if there was another life beckoning. Now 23 years old, he'd been an AFL prospect who never played in the AFL, and a warrior who'd seen no real combat. Maybe it was time just to be Joe Blow.

CHAPTER SIX

THE ECHO OF GUNS

'He really did try to make it in civilian life.'

IAN TURNER

SYDNEY, NEW SOUTH WALES
2004

Cam had completed his four-year commitment to the Army: perhaps it was time to live a regular life? He and Robin had already moved in together, so he started thinking that perhaps he should get a regular job, build a home and forget his dreams of an extraordinary life.

Cameron and seven other commandos left 4RAR within one week. Six were from Bravo Company. Although each soldier had his own reasons, the disorganisation of the Iraq deployment had been a contributing factor for all of them.

For many, another factor had been their exposure, in Iraq, to the work done by private contractors – usually former American green berets, SEALs and other special forces alumni – who were winning lucrative contracts from both private and public entities.

'There was this massive war roaring and at 4RAR we're doing absolutely fuck all,' says Ian 'Turns' Turner, one of the soldiers who left 4RAR at the same time as Cam. 'Heaps of us felt like we'd been left behind. I was one of the first to leave and go over to Iraq to work as a contractor, and the word filtered back pretty quickly that the work was available.'

Numbers had been exchanged, and promises of very lucrative contracts given. If the commandos' extensive training wasn't going to be used fully as a tool of Australian foreign policy, then perhaps it could be used to earn some private security contracts in Iraq. Australian soldiers weren't the only ones thinking that way; for special forces soldiers around the world, this period became known as 'The Bonanza'.

The eight commandos who had asked to leave the unit were called up in front of the Regimental Sergeant Major

(RSM), the highest-ranking enlisted soldier in 4RAR, and the man in charge of discipline and standards within the unit. 'Don't think that you blokes will be able to go over there, earn your money and then just come back afterwards,' he barked at them. 'It's not going to work like that. If you're out, you're out.'

For a unit like 4RAR, this exodus of men was a calamity. Losing even one highly trained soldier was disappointing; losing eight in a week was verging on a crisis. Soldiers like Cameron Baird, who had combat experience and endless course certifications, weren't forged cheaply or easily.

The departing men suspected the RSM's threat was an empty one, but even if it wasn't, they didn't care. Iraq would soon be conquered, or so they thought, and the Taliban was about to fold, or so they thought, and they'd not been trusted to get into the kind of fighting they'd trained so hard for. It seemed the opportunity for direct-action warfare was gone. Some decided they would return to Iraq to cash in on 'The Bonanza'; others chose to give civilian life a go. Almost all would eventually return, drawn as if by sirens' song to the gunfire echoing along Afghanistan's valleys.

Peace isn't for everyone.

—

Eddie Robertson was one of the eight men who left Bravo with Cam, and after leaving he was soon employed by the Iraqi Electoral Commission. He was working alongside a number of former 4RAR guys, and says the experience of being a contractor was in stark contrast to their military deployment.

While in Iraq, 4RAR was insulated somewhat from the madness of post-Saddam Iraq, but contractors had no such luxury. They had to be the bulwark against the jagged edges of a broken society. In fact, one of the first indicators that the Iraqi insurgency was in full swing was when four military contractors drove to a city they believed to have been conquered, Fallujah, and were ambushed, their bodies dragged down the street and hung on a bridge spanning the Euphrates.

Afterwards, the city descended into open warfare, with US soldiers fighting their first battle against the group that would later metastasise into ISIS. The insurgents surprised the Americans, fighting them to a bloody stalemate. Eddie Robertson was not working in Fallujah, but his stories still tell of a wholly damaged country. On one occasion, in the course of his everyday work, a man tried to sell him a T-72 battle tank. Eddie visited the Iraqi man's house, in the north of the country, and saw that not only had this man procured a fully operational battle tank, he had it in his backyard. Eddie told the man that he was good for tanks.

The danger for military contractors was not only physical, but moral. Until 2008, the contractors were operating outside of Iraqi law, codified by Coalition Provisional Authority Order Number 17.

In 2006 I met two New Zealand contractors who worked for a company called Kellogg Brown & Root on a Multi-National Force (MNF) base in the south of Iraq, who casually told me about finding two prepubescent boys trying to set an improvised explosive device (IED), and executing them. Whether the story was true or not, it spoke to the impunity with which contractors felt they could work. The private military contractors were killing, and they were being killed. The moral standard was variable, and the combat support minimal.

It was in these conditions that Cam Baird decided to take a private military contracting job. Doug says that Cam was 24 hours away from leaving Sydney, with his bags packed and a contract and ticket in his hand. The family were worried and got together to explain their concerns to him.

'We never felt uncomfortable with him going to East Timor or Iraq [with the Army] but we did feel uncomfortable about the idea of him doing that,' says Doug Baird.

'There was no structure whatsoever. If shit happens, then you just gotta try to get out of it yourself. We said, as strongly as we could, that we didn't want him to go.'

Kaye said that it took some time for her to get used to the idea of Cam being a soldier, but she did get there. Now, she told Cam she didn't think she'd ever be comfortable with the idea of him being a private military contractor.

Just a few hours before he was set to leave, Cam called his parents to tell them that he was staying in Sydney.

'He must have already had some doubts, though,' Kaye says, 'because if he really had made his mind up, we wouldn't have stopped him from going.'

It's likely that Robin was another dissenting voice. Cam was always reticent to talk to others about private conversations the pair had, but she'd articulated to others that she was happy he had left the military, so it's unlikely she'd want him in Iraq as a contractor.

'He wasn't dirty that he didn't go, though,' says Turns, who had also left Bravo Company but did go to Iraq as a contractor. 'He really did try to make it in civilian life.'

Cam picked up two jobs in this period, one a day job and the other a night job. The day job was as a security guard in Sydney's Darling Harbour, which mostly kept him in a chair in a booth all day, watching television screens.

The night job was as a bouncer, working the leagues clubs of western Sydney and the nightclubs of Kings Cross.

Cam never complained to his friends about either job, but he did mention that the day job was unexciting, while the night job awakened the lesser angels of his personality. He enjoyed it, perhaps a little too much, whenever a group of drunken men tried to fight him.

'He told me he didn't mind the bouncing,' says Chris Dyer. 'The bouncers would always have these dickheads thinking they were tough, and I think Cam laid a few of them out.'

Perhaps the job fed the aggression that had been instilled in Cam by his infantry training. It could only ever be a pale substitute to combat, however.

Another detraction of both jobs was that there was no progression – nothing to learn. There is no such thing as a 'finished' special forces soldier, however; there's always a new threat profile, a new TTP (techniques, tactics and procedure), a new weaponry system, a new air platform, a new FE (force element) to integrate. Keeping up with the acronyms was a task in itself. The endless lessons of that job had been something that Cam truly loved – and now that was gone.

It seems that, with Robin, Cam did try to discover a sense of progression. The pair went through a papier-mâché stage, a bread-making phase and endless home-improvement projects. There was also a horticultural stage. One time Ian Turner bumped into Cam on the train and noticed immediately that Cam was carrying a bonsai tree. 'He had his bike with him,' he recalls, 'and a little saddle bag full of VB throwdowns [250 ml bottles of beer] and he said he was on his way to North Sydney to talk to a bloke about a tiny tree. I said, "Righto, mate." I mean, he was always into the most random shit.'

Cam and Robin also started visiting Buddhist temples and meditating. There are hints, throughout his life, that Cam often wondered about spirituality, and especially Eastern spirituality. He did yoga at school, and meditated. He read books by modern philosophers such as Alain de Botton and Ram Dass. He read the Qur'an and Salman Rushdie's novel *The Satanic Verses*, which had so enraged the theocratic leaders of Iran that they issued a fatwa calling for the writer's death.

Cam tried to build a life of significance with Robin, one that had nothing to do with carrying a gun overseas. This life was to include marriage.

Cam called Kaye first, to tell his mum that he was planning to pop the question.

'Why do you want to do that?' Kaye asked.

Her reaction had nothing to do with Robin; Kaye just thought marriage was a bit of an antiquated notion for someone so young.

'I want to make a commitment,' Cam told her.

Kaye said that if that was what he wanted to do, then she was very happy for him.

Doug was happy also. Cam and Robin had visited Kaye and Doug's home many times now, and he'd only ever seen them as a very content and caring couple. There was an age difference, but love and care was all that mattered in a relationship, as far as Doug was concerned.

Brendan organised the buck's night. A number of Cam's mates from school were flying up to Sydney for the wedding, so the party was planned for the night before the nuptials. Cam had arranged, through his bouncing connections, for his mates' names to be on the door at the Cargo Bar, then a relatively exclusive bar in Darling Harbour.

Cam's schoolmates Daniel Carroll, Rick Green and Chris Dyer were particularly excited, not only because they were having a boozy night out in Sydney, but also because they were having a boozy night with Cam – their first ever.

'For all of us it was our first buck's, and we were in Sydney at this schmick bar and we're all like, "Here we go,"' says Daniel Carroll.

Then, to their great chagrin, Cam arrived late and left early.

'We were playing pool and he turned up and we're like, "Here we go," but he just went nuts on the beers for a little bit and then left,' says Carroll.

Where Cam went was anyone's guess. Both the Army and Melbourne contingents kept the revelry going deep into the Kings Cross night, with Brendan leading the charge.

The next day Cam and Robin got married at a pretty little church in the outer-Sydney suburb of Narellan. It was quite a small affair, and when Robin walked down the aisle she walked alone, as both her parents had already passed away. When Cam saw his bride, he broke down crying. He regained his composure and, after saying I do, he threw a rock sign to the onlookers. The reception was held at a nearby RSL, and Cam and Robin entered the party with AC/DC blasting.

After the wedding and years of living in rented houses, the pair decided to build a home in Mount Annan. Their life seemed settled. And then the Special Operations Task Group (SOTG) rotations began in Afghanistan. The sound of guns and bombs could faintly be heard in Sydney. Cam's mates were re-enlisting. The gravity of war started to pull at Cameron Baird. He had a decision to make.

Both a back injury and a lack of opportunity for combat had pushed Cam to leave the Army, but things had changed. He had been running regularly and, at work, had even managed to chase down and tackle a man who was trying to jimmy open an ATM. His back now felt fine, strong even, with the pain all but gone. Cam Baird had no doubt that he was physically capable of returning to the commandos. The opportunity for combat had also presented itself too.

The Australian Special Operations Command was in the process of undertaking a monumental task, one that would require a complete revitalisation. The greatest changes were happening at Holsworthy. 4RAR would become the fully realised special forces unit that it had been envisioned as, and more. The commando unit was at last about to have its trial by fire. All of a sudden, the unit needed Cam – and he needed it.

CHAPTER SEVEN

BACK TO BRAVO

'At least you're not going to Iraq.'

KAYE BAIRD

In the wake of the 9/11 attacks, the United States had unprecedented international and domestic support in attacking al-Qaeda and the Taliban, and their attack on Afghanistan in October 2001 was an unmitigated success. The full force of the world's most potent military was unleashed on perhaps the most backward regime in the world, and the results were what one would expect.

For a while the Taliban fought the coalition advance with conventional warfare methods, digging into defensive positions in Kabul, but these proved completely useless against their opponents with their massive technological superiority. With complete control of the air, and ground armaments that were exponentially more powerful than anything the Taliban could bring to bear, the coalition essentially had only to choose a fixed target before, moments later, it would disappear into a cloud of dust.

This initial phase of the Afghanistan War can be best summarised by something US Secretary of Defense Donald Rumsfeld said to the press, just two days after the war had started: 'We're not running out of targets, Afghanistan is.' Even as Rumsfeld spoke, CIA operators and American special forces soldiers had started linking up with Afghan opposition fighters. Pundits were already speculating that this would be a very short and very inexpensive war.

A few months later, the United States and their coalition partners, including Australia, got a taste of what the thirteen-year, multi-trillion-dollar war was really going to be like.

Australia had announced a commitment of special forces soldiers to the Afghanistan War in October 2001, and it took two months for 1 Squadron SASR to arrive in the country. By the end of February 2002, Australia had suffered its first combat casualty, and the first Australian military death in action since Vietnam: a Long Range Patrol Vehicle (LRPV) hit an anti-vehicle mine, killing 33-year-old Sergeant Andrew Russell.

In March 2002, more than 80 men from 1 Squadron were called in to be part of a mission called Operation Anaconda. Notable US war historian Andrew J. Bacevich has said the US planners of Anaconda envisioned it being something of a 'grouse hunt'. Blocking forces were to seal the north and south entrances of the Shah-i-Kot Valley, which would allow American soldiers to drop into the valley and pick up or kill a large number of the al-Qaeda or Taliban high-value targets (HVTs) who were believed to be there. It was, by some estimations, the mission that would end the war.

The fighting was far more extreme than anyone had envisioned, though, and the operation's assets were stretched to the limit. Hundreds more al-Qaeda and Taliban fighters presented themselves for battle than were expected. US helicopters were shot down, and American positions nearly overrun. Afghans evaded detection from multi-million-dollar aerial optical systems by hiding under fog or the canopy of trees. When they no longer wanted to fight, they would break the cordon and melt away, later disappearing across the porous border with Pakistan, or into the tribal south of the country. No HVTs were captured or killed.

The SASR had played some small but vital roles in Anaconda, gaining particular notice when they defended a group of US Army Rangers who were in danger of being overrun after their helicopter was shot down. Senior American military and civilian voices went out of their way to praise the SASR's work, and that, no doubt, contributed to the Australian special forces units' expanded role in southern Afghanistan a few years later.

Although Operation Anaconda is now seen as a cautionary tale detailing the difficulties of securing Afghanistan, at the time it was thought to be nothing more than an aberration in the inexorable journey towards completion of the mission. Keen to move the focus to Iraq, the United States made every effort to frame Anaconda as a rousing success, and perhaps even as the full stop in the conflict they had envisioned it as.

In the wake of Anaconda, a coalition-approved *loya jirga,* or grand assembly, established a new interim government for Afghanistan, with Hamid Karzai, a notable anti-Taliban politician, as president. The Americans were pleased to begin preparing to cede responsibility for the country back to the Afghan people.

The SASR element returned to Australia in November 2002, and in May 2003 Secretary Rumsfeld declared an end to 'major combat' in Afghanistan. Military support of the Afghan government was now the responsibility of the NATO-led International Security Assistance Force (ISAF), and the eyes of the world moved to Iraq, where a show-down with Saddam Hussein beckoned.

But there were still embers in that Afghan fire. In fact, there were all the conditions for a blaze. As there were not many more than 10 000 US troops deployed in Afghanistan at the time of the invasion of Iraq (compared to the 100 000 troops that would be there by 2010), the Taliban quickly began to reconstitute and consolidate – and not just the Taliban, but dozens of other armed, anti-government groups as well, including Afghanistan's powerful narco-barons.

Incapable of projecting much force out into the country-side, and unable to seal the border with tribal Pakistan, the new Afghan government and ISAF started to lose control of huge swathes of the country, especially in the Pashtun south. There, tribal alliances and a tradition of opium production drove the populace into the arms of anti-government forces, and especially the resurgent Taliban, largely a Pashtun organisation.

ISAF and the Afghan government (but mostly ISAF) developed a plan to pacify the country by quadrants, working counter-clockwise from Kabul. In each of the four stages, ISAF would install international forces, relieve the meagre US military presence, and set up 'government in a box' Provincial Reconstruction Teams (PRTs). In 2004 and

2005, stages one and two sent Canadian and European troops to the relatively peaceful north and west. Then came the all-important stage three, which required taking control of the violent southern provinces of Helmand and Kandahar. This was where the toughest fighting would happen: it would likely be the hinge on which success would turn.

A number of nations had contributed to ISAF, but most had put caveats on their deployments that kept them from being able to efficiently operate in the south of Afghanistan. Spanish and Italian troops were discouraged from combat operations, while German troops wouldn't leave their base at night. One ISAF country wouldn't fight after snow had fallen; another wouldn't allow Afghans on its helicopters. It would therefore be difficult for these nations to operate in the country's most volatile provinces, where it was expected there would be casualties and an exceptional amount of kinetic combat, both defensive and offensive. To work effectively in the south, substantial special forces units were essential.

In 2005 Australia's defence minister, Robert Hill, announced that the nation's forces were back working operationally in Afghanistan. He later declared that his government was committing a larger force as ISAF rolled out its four-stage plan to wrest back control of the Afghan countryside. Australia had agreed to take on a significant role in the province of Uruzgan, an area bordering both Kandahar and Helmand, the two provinces in which the Taliban had the strongest grasp. Uruzgan was a small province – its population was not much larger than Canberra's – but it was strategically important, with Taliban 'rat lines' running through it, linking the southern regions with Kabul.

Along with other units, Australia was deploying a SOTG to Uruzgan. This would include SASR operators and engineers from the Incident Response Regiment (IRR), but also a large number of commandos from 4RAR. In time, the regiment would undertake 20 gruelling rotations in Afghanistan. These 'rots', each lasting between four and seven months, would become central in the unit's story, in many ways coming to define it. As one commando told me, Vietnam was the making of the SASR, but Afghanistan was to be the making of Australia's full-time commando unit.

—

Undertaken by 4RAR's Alpha Company, Rotation One (Rot One) was largely about establishing an Australian camp in the tiny provincial backwater capital of Tarin Kowt. Sitting inside the site of American Forward Operating Base (FOB) Ripley, Camp Russell – named after the SASR operator killed in 2002 – was adjacent to the US base and the Dutch base, Kamp Holland. Soldiers on this initial rotation spent little time outside the wire and saw almost no combat.

Rot Two was undertaken by Bravo Company, and they were the first commandos to start to project force into the valleys and plains around Tarin Kowt. As one commando put it, that rotation got into 'a few small little stinks', especially as they scouted routes into the nearby 'red' (or enemy-controlled) Chora Valley. The Rot Two operations, however, opened the door for a Rot Three, which would involve the heaviest fighting any Australian military force had seen since Vietnam.

In December 2005 the new Afghan government sat for the first time and was instantly confronted by a resurgent Taliban. Not only had parts of the south become no-go zones for the government, there were indications that the Taliban now had a capacity to move north whenever they chose, with suicide bombings and guerrilla attacks in Kabul and nearby population centres on the rise.

It was believed that, if peace was to come to the north, the south would have to be pacified. To that end, ISAF planned a huge, division-sized assault on Taliban strongholds across the south. Named Operation Mountain Thrust, the mission smashed through valleys and plains across Helmand and Kandahar in mid-2006, killing more than 1000 Taliban fighters and ostensibly creating the conditions for ISAF to gain a foothold in those provinces.

As Operation Mountain Thrust started to wind down, a smaller Australian version of the mission, Operation Perth, began. It was to concentrate on pacifying the Chora Valley, which was only about 40 kilometres from Camp Russell, but still very much impassable for the reconstruction teams. It was from here that the Taliban were believed to be launching many of their attacks in the region.

Confident in their capacity, Operation Perth essentially had coalition forces present themselves in the valley for a fight, daring the opposition to rise to the challenge. The decision would be the Taliban fighters' to make: would they fight for what they considered theirs, or would they accept that there was a new order?

The fighting started almost as soon as the coalition force entered the valley. Before the mission began, the Aussie LRPVs were laden with ammunition for mortars, heavy machine guns and Javelin launchers. Six days later, the supplies were all but spent, and two AC-130 Spectre gunships supporting the troops on the ground had completely emptied the magazines of their gun platforms.

The operation ended after nine days, and while there were wounded Australians, they had suffered no fatalities.

The Taliban had many hundreds of casualties, including an estimated 150 dead.

Special forces soldiers from the Dutch Korps Commandotroepen (KCT), the American Green Berets and the New Zealand SAS had taken part in the fighting, but the bulk of the force was Australian, with most of the triggermen coming from 4RAR. It was a huge moment for the commandos. After almost a decade of preparation, the unit had finally been unleashed on the battlefield.

It was during this mission, one commando told me, that the unit learned about the moral difficulties of fighting in Afghanistan. This man described spotting, in his gunsights, a child of 10 or 11 who was ferrying rounds to an insurgent mortar team. After firing warning shots at the boy's feet and over his head, the commando had to aim mid-chest. 'I was fucked up, but that was the job,' he said. 'If it was them or my mates, it was always going to be them.'

There was a long gap between Rot Three and Rot Four, with almost the entire SOTG demobilising and heading back to Australia. After Operation Perth, it was believed in Canberra that the Australian area of operations (AO) had largely been pacified, and that security could now be undertaken by other regular units. That belief was wildly wrong.

After a few months without the SOTG, Australian operations outside of Tarin Kowt were regularly subjected to insurgent attack. The overall mission was moving onto the back foot; soon the Australians would be unable to undertake the reconstruction missions they were there to do.

The SOTG returned to Uruzgan. They would be tasked with confronting the Taliban head-on, in order both to take the pressure off the other Australian forces, and to kill or capture insurgent leaders. The war the commandos wanted was finally there for them.

—

The guys who had left the unit after Iraq heard all of this. About Uruzgan and Tarin Kowt, about Operation Perth, and about the pause in rotations and the resumption. Almost all who had left Bravo Company after Iraq started to filter back to Holsworthy to re-enlist. Eddie Robertson and Ian Turner returned within weeks of each other. Not long after them, Cameron Baird arrived.

In August 2006 he told Robin he was going back to the unit, and on 12 September he re-enlisted. With the unit at war and desperate for competent, experienced soldiers, Cam, Eddie and Ian were welcomed back. The RSM's threats had indeed proven empty. Cam would be required to serve at least another four years, but he was now looking further ahead than that.

'He was a rejuvenated soldier and was very career-minded now,' says his brother, Brendan.

Kaye was concerned about Cam going back into the service, and she knew he was likely to be sent to Afghanistan. 'At least you're not going to Iraq,' she told him.

At that time, Iraq was on the verge of going to hell in a handbasket, and the fight against the Taliban had barely started. With only one Australian combat death sustained in Afghanistan so far, the public perception was that Australian forces would be tucked away in a peace-keeping role. Cam didn't tell his mother that wasn't going to be the case.

'He knew he was going to be right in the middle of the fighting,' says Brendan, 'and when he got back all he wanted to do was gain as much competency as possible.'

Willy Lacquer, a commando who would end up in Cameron Baird's assault team, remembers the first day Cam arrived back at Holsworthy. 'He had this swagger, and I was like, "Who's this big unit come out of nowhere?" Turns out everyone knew who he was. There were a lot of stories going around.'

Cam was close to being one of the originals of 4RAR. Still just 24 years old, he was as young as or younger than most of the men who had joined the unit since he'd left, but he was considered a veteran. He was reinstalled back at Bravo Company, which hosted most of the post-Iraq 're-treads'. The company's next rotation, into Afghanistan, would be in August 2007, so Cam joined a number of blokes who were racing against the calendar to tick off all their competency checks so they could go into the 'reo' cycle and be eligible for deployment.

Despite having been out for almost two years, Cameron wasn't too far behind many of the men in Bravo, especially the junior soldiers. The unit was set to undertake a huge transformation in its skills base over the coming years, but to this point not too much had changed.

The main difference was in how the unit conducted close-quarters combat operations. While Cam was a civilian, most of the guys in Bravo had spent a year working in TAG (East). In that counter-terrorism role, they'd done a lot of compound and facility assault training. This close-quarters battle training was somewhat different from the kinds of assaults the unit would be conducting in Afghanistan – TAG training had a greater focus on hostage rescue – but it did improve the soldiers' skills in clearing rooms and compounds cooperatively, something they would have to do time and again in Afghanistan. As one of the soldiers told me, the main thing they had taken out of 'black role' was the confidence not to accidentally shoot one of your own blokes.

Two back-to-back Advanced Close Quarters Battle courses were organised for those Bravo soldiers who hadn't served in TAG (East). The course included a 'package' of pistol and rifle shooting drills, then door-entrance drilling and different room-clearance scenarios. Like a team of dancers, the soldiers were initially uncoordinated and had to think about every move, but at the end of the seven-week course they worked in unison, moving through rooms as one entity.

The course had a strong focus on night compound clearances, as night assaults were to be used tactically in Afghanistan. Most Taliban fighters were unequipped with night-vision goggles (although some senior Taliban had older sets), giving the Australians an advantage; also, the commandos would frequently be working in environments where there was no artificial lighting.

In the weeks leading up to deployment, Bravo drilled hard on specific scenarios thought to be likely to occur in Afghanistan, such as road clearance and vehicle recovery (even though the IED plague was yet to take hold in Uruzgan). They also began receiving specific briefings about the theatre of war they were about to enter.

The men were told that Uruzgan is a poor, arid province, mostly covered by treeless mountains. The locals lived among those mountains, by the rivers that irrigated their fields of potato, maize, apricots and rice. Literacy rates were very low, and infant mortality was high among both the Pashtun people, who mostly lived in the countryside, and the Hazara people, who were more numerous in the provincial capital, Tarin Kowt. The Kochi people, a nomadic group, roamed throughout the province.

Until 2006 the province had been run by Jan Mohammad Khan, an ally of Hamid Karzai and also likely a producer and trafficker of opium. Khan had been an agitator in local politics since his dismissal from the governorship, and the soldiers were told this would likely continue. His nephew Matiullah Khan was a rising force in the region, and a man the commandos should be aware of. Formerly the head of the Highway Police, Matiullah Khan's unit was disbanded when his uncle was deposed, but he retained a large and relatively effective militia. He was also likely an opium trafficker. Both the Khans were opposed to the Taliban, however, and so were warily considered friends of Australia.

Bravo Company's final pre-deployment training was undertaken at a military base in Woomera, in the north of South Australia. There the company alternated between drilling and live-fire exercises. On the last night in South Australia, there was an almighty piss-up. Details concerning this night are not available, but I'm told Bravo is no longer welcome to train at Woomera.

Command elements in the unit made their way to Tarin Kowt in preparation for the arrival of the larger force, but most of the commandos had ten days of leave before they were deployed. Although the average age of the unit was just 25, many of the soldiers were married, so they spent the next week and a half at home with their partners.

Cameron Baird had a quiet week and a half with Robin, and then reported back to Holsworthy. He was chomping at the bit for his first taste of real warfare.

CHAPTER EIGHT

DEATH IN CHENARTU

'It's Afghanistan, mate. What the fuck did you expect?'

CAMERON BAIRD

TARIN KOWT, AFGHANISTAN
2007–08

In mid-2007 Cam Baird and the men of Bravo Company were put on buses and taken to Sydney airport. With relaxed grooming protocols in effect, many of the guys were already growing the beards that are almost a prerequisite for special forces soldiers on deployment. Most were wearing Merrell Moab boots, commonly used in place of the Army's standard-issue boots. Cam was an exception: he rarely wore anything that wasn't Army-issue.

Although the commandos were supposed to be incognito at the airport, one only had to look at them to know, as Eddie Robertson says, they were 'obviously not a footy team'.

They boarded a 'Strategic Airlines' Airbus in Sydney, and, after a quick stopover at a base in the Indian Ocean, landed in the Middle East. They were ferried quickly from the airport to Camp Buehring, an American facility which one US Army public affairs officer described as being 'like Las Vegas'. For a few days the men of Bravo Company watched movies and played video games in the huge 'Morale, Welfare and Recreation' hall, chowed down on the vast array of American fast food available in 'Fat Alley', stocked up on weapons and armaments, and waited for their turn on the 'brown route' – the nonstop flight to Tarin Kowt (commonly known as TK). Finally, they loaded up into C-130 transports and were away.

When Cam Baird arrived in Tarin Kowt, he found it to be a place of contrasts. Camp Russell was all plywood, HESCO bastions and temporary containers, while the adjacent town was filled with the simple and unpleasant man-made structures typical of a small third-world provincial capital. Dust covered everything, fine like talcum powder. Beyond the town, though, craggy mountains jutted out of the horizon. Dusted white in winter and brown, red and yellow in summer, they suggested something beguiling, and mysterious.

What lay beyond those mountains, in many directions, was a fight waiting to happen, red on a map, and the spot where Bravo Company would suffer its first combat casualty.

Bravo and Alpha companies were briefly in camp together while responsibilities were handed over, and most Bravo soldiers sought out their Alpha brethren to get an unofficial man-to-man briefing on what they should expect when they got outside the wire. Rot Five would have similar goals to Rot Four: pressuring the supply lines that ran through Uruzgan, as well as attacking Taliban infrastructure and hitting local commanders and bomb makers as they revealed themselves.

While on the base, the soldiers were also briefed on the JPEL, or Joint Prioritized Effects List, a coalition-wide (and sometimes contentious) catalogue of Taliban leaders who were to be captured or killed, should intelligence about their whereabouts become available. At some points during the war the list had up to 750 names on it, as well as their region, tribal affiliation, priority and (in some cases) the US Department of Defense reward for their killing.

A few days after arriving in Tarin Kowt, it was finally time for Bravo to get outside the wire. The commandos' first mission was to be an eventful one.

It was supposed to be a 'nursery patrol', a drive through a relatively safe area, so the incoming soldiers could get some experience in the vehicles and communications under Afghan conditions. This patrol would include both platoons of the company, moving out in LRPVs, thin-skinned, open-top vehicles armed with mounted machine guns and Mk 19 grenade launchers. The men would speak to locals, get some intel and return unharmed.

That was the plan, anyway.

—

There would be three men in each vehicle, and two vehicles per team. As the 2IC of his team, Cam was responsible for the men in his car. As well as checking navigation and ensuring that his team was where it should be, Cam was tasked with relaying information to his team commander.

The patrol began as expected. The team covered a good amount of ground at a decent clip, spoke to locals when they could and began to get a sense of the mood on the ground. On the way back to Tarin Kowt, in a valley just a few kilometres from the base, Cam's platoon spotted a group of Kochi nomads in a green belt, grass-covered land close to a river. Historically, the Kochi did not get involved in insurgency, and because they moved around every corner of Uruzgan, it was thought it might be useful to talk to them about any Taliban activity they had noticed.

One of the platoons set up in a defensive position, where the pass to the valley and the high ground could be covered by guns, and a foot patrol, including Cam and an interpreter, was sent down to the green belt. While they were speaking to the nomads, a call came over the radio advising that Taliban fighters were planning to attack the Australian patrol. This wasn't the first claim of an imminent ambush: the enemy knew the Australians could listen to their communications, and they liked to try to spook the soldiers. As this was the nursery patrol, however, the decision was made to send the foot patrol back to the vehicles, and the vehicles back to TK.

Before the foot patrol could make their way back to the vehicles, the commando snipers spotted Taliban fighters approaching and began firing at them with their rifles and mortars. Most of the soldiers in the foot patrol thought it was unlikely that this would amount to much of an attack. It was the middle of the day and the Taliban usually preferred to fight at first or last light; moreover, this Australian force was a company-sized element, a hell of a lot for the Taliban to deal with.

But as the foot patrol got closer to their vehicles, they started taking in enemy rounds.

While Cam's platoon had been speaking to the Kochi people, the other platoon had been drilling on the river. When the fighting started, they loaded back into their vehicles, joined up with the company headquarters element and moved to a ridgeline so they could cover the movement of Cam's platoon.

While they waited, the static platoon was relaxed. There'd been a bit of shooting and excitement, but everything they knew convinced them that this was not a concerted Taliban ambush. As time passed, Tim Stanton, another commando roughly the same age as Cam, fished out of his pocket a packet of Skittles that he'd been saving. He nestled himself into his seat in the LRPV, opened the packet and reached for the paperback he'd been reading: Giacomo Casanova's memoir, *Histoire de Ma Vie*. Then, he says, 'the whole world erupted'.

Both Baird's platoon and Stanton's started receiving wave after wave of small-arms and machine-gun fire, as well as rocket-propelled grenades and mortar rounds. The two platoons linked up and, after returning fire, began to move out of the effective range of the Taliban attack.

Electronic counter-measures (ECM) were engaged against the Taliban, but Cam's role as vehicle commander became increasingly difficult, as equipment issues interrupted his communications. Eddie, who was in the vehicle with Cam on this patrol, says Cameron was unfazed: the 2IC kept as complete a picture of the battle plan as he could with the comms he had, relayed messages to the team leader as he requested them, and fed ammunition to the vehicle's gunner as he covered their retreat.

When they were almost a kilometre away from the initial contact, the undamaged vehicles positioned their guns towards the enemy element as the damaged cars were put up on jacks for repairs.

'When we were set up I remember thinking, *An Afghan would have to be crazy to stick his head up and shoot at a whole company lined up like this*,' Tim Stanton remembers. 'Then . . .'

More effective fire started coming in, with a hail of armour-piercing rounds starting to punch into the thin-skinned vehicles.

The company commander and platoon commander decided to move to a high feature, where they could pinpoint their position and plan their return to TK. Once there, both men were shot – one through the calf, the other in the buttocks. Neither needed evacuation; the only permanent injury was to their pride.

'I mean, infantry 101, you don't stand on top of a fucking mountain with a map spread out,' says Stanton. 'They reckon they got targeted by a sniper, but I'm pretty sure it was just some dude going, "Look at those fuck-heads," and spraying some rounds their way. Everyone thought they knew shit about fighting then, but now we know we had no clue. We had no idea what Afghan was about yet.'

Air support was called in, and the hills from which the Taliban rounds were emanating were painted with fire. When the vehicles were repaired and the commanders treated, the convoy slowly made a fighting retreat back to TK. When fire came in to the vehicles it was returned, augmented by Joint Direct Action Munition (JDAM) bombs.

It was the first time most of the commandos had seen bombs like that in the field. Most say they were impressed at the time, but now some wonder how effective the munitions were, with the Taliban disappearing into fighting holes dug after the Soviet invasion. It's likely most of the attackers had never known a time of peace in their lives, but for most of the defenders it was their first experience of combat.

When the patrol got back to TK, the damage was tallied. Many of the LRPVs were riddled with bullet holes. Javelin anti-tank missiles stored on the side of the vehicles had been shot, and the butt of one of the mounted rifles had been pierced. The holes told a tale of close calls; there was a general sense of wonderment that none of the soldiers on the patrol had been killed.

'It's embarrassing to say, but it was a fucking shambles,' says Stanton. 'They owned the fuck out of us that day.'

Back at TK, Eddie started wondering what the next five months had in store for them. 'Is it going to be like this all the time?' he asked Cam as they re-stocked their vehicle with food and ammunition.

'It's Afghanistan, mate,' said Cam. 'What the fuck did you expect?'

Cam spoke to his brother after the deployment and said that patrol was not only what he'd expected, but what he'd wanted. He had not been scared, agitated or excited by the combat. Cam had been preparing for moments like these ever since he joined the Army.

After that patrol, the jobs started coming in regularly for Bravo, but they were less dramatic. Mostly Bravo men were tasked with raiding compounds suspected of hosting insurgents, but usually they found only farmers and the weapons that one might expect in any village in rural Afghanistan.

—

The Taliban were there, though. The commandos could hear them on the radios, and every so often would find the litter of their camps, or the traps and explosives they left on the road. They were definitely in the area; they just weren't engaging.

Then the commandos were summoned for a job named Operation Detachment. In central Uruzgan there was an American outpost called Firebase Anaconda. Manned mostly by Green Berets, the base had been under nightly attack from mortars and rockets. The American force had been planning to undertake missions outside the wire to win back the initiative, but most of their efforts had to be dedicated to base security. Firebase Anaconda was one of the few coalition installations where the Taliban had attempted a full-frontal attack.

Bravo was tasked with moving up to Anaconda with vehicles, relieving the Green Berets inside, conducting some offensive disruption operations, and rolling out again – by which time the Americans would hopefully be back on the front foot. Once again, Cam was a vehicle commander for the trip. Here he would learn just how difficult even a seemingly simple task could be in Afghanistan.

As the crow flies, Firebase Anaconda was just a couple of hundred kilometres from Camp Russell. Even allowing for the perilous roads, the drive was estimated to take roughly 12 hours. Only a few hours into the drive, though, it became apparent that it was going to take far longer.

The road was supposed to be sealed in some parts, but was not. It seemed the force was constantly having to stop for repairs, or to dislodge a vehicle from a ditch, and each time they'd have to establish a security perimeter. Such activities burned the hours away.

At one point an Afghan military Hilux rolled over, and when it couldn't be righted the convoy had to wait for an AC-130 Spectre gunship to arrive. The vehicle and its sensitive communications equipment had to be destroyed from the air.

After that stop, there was constant chatter on the radio from nearby Taliban fighters about an imminent attack. They liked to verbally threaten and harass coalition patrols, regardless of whether they were actually planning to follow through. Translators would interpret the messages: 'Abdul, bring the watermelons; we need them to give to the infidels. The big watermelons. They are very hungry . . .'

To discourage a Taliban attack, an A-10 Warthog fighter jet in the vicinity was called in to fly low over the patrol as a show of force. One of the Bravo boys managed to raise the pilot on the radio to pass on their thanks for the attention; he was surprised to find a female voice telling him not to mention it.

Cam Baird and Bravo got to Firebase Anaconda almost 30 hours after leaving their base. After setting up a security plan and getting some chow, the soldiers were told to take 12 hours of rest before getting ready for night operations.

Cam and Eddie took themselves to a watering hole that the Americans had dug on the base, before wedging themselves under their vehicles for a bit of much-needed shut-eye. Their sleep was a restless one, however, as they were both often woken by the boom of a 120 mm mortar the Americans had set up in the middle of the base.

That night, operations began. Under a veil of darkness and with the element of surprise, the Australians hit compound after compound. A few small gunfights ensued, and a small number of weapons and explosives were found, but that wasn't really the goal of having the 4RAR operating out of Anaconda. It was to give the Green Berets the opportunity to conduct a series of operations that they deemed necessary if they were to gain ascendancy in the area; the details are still classified.

Ten days later, the Australian forces were recalled to their TK base; of course, it was once again a slow passage. When they were nearly back, a group of Afghan kids approached the vehicles with their hands out, looking for some free stationery or items from the soldiers' Meals Ready to Eat (MREs).

Along the way, Eddie and Cam, like the other commandos, had given out chocolate bars and pens to kids they'd seen along the route. Now they had nothing left, so Eddie grabbed some little bottles of Tabasco sauce that were in the American-made MREs. The kids began pouring the hot sauce straight into their mouths.

'Eddie, they're not going to like that,' Cam said. 'They're gonna go and tell their big brothers and we're going to be in the shit.'

The comedy of the moment was heightened by Cam's headwear, a black plastic cowboy hat that the boys had bought at a local market.

Shortly after the laughing ended, an ambush began. First, accurate small-arms fire peppered the convoy, with rocket-propelled grenade (RPG) rounds coming in shortly afterwards. Cam returned fire with a look of determination under a brim of black plastic, popping off high-explosive rounds from his underslung M203 grenade launcher, augmenting the fire that was coming from the vehicle's Mk 19.

The engagement was ended with the help of a Canadian special forces unit, which rained down accurate mortar fire onto the Afghan attackers, but not before Eddie and Cam's vehicle had to stop for some close-quarters fighting when their Mk 19 jammed.

With the vehicle stopped, Cam and Eddie were shoulder to shoulder, scanning the ground for threats as the Mk 19 was worked on. Cam saw a Taliban fighter pop up with an RPG over Eddie's shoulder, and swung the vehicle's MAG 58 next to Eddie's ear, dropping the enemy with a tight burst of fire.

'You fucking cunt!' Eddie hollered, unable to hear his own words. 'I'm deaf!'

Under the brim of his absurd hat, Cam smiled and gave Eddie his apologies. They drove back to the base without further incident.

—

Later in the rotation, the Bravo men were sometimes greeted by a huge experimental mine-clearing vehicle, which they knew variously as 'the Chubby', 'that pile of shit' or occasionally the Husky Vehicle Mounted Mine Detector (VMMD).

One night an inexperienced Chubby operator was guiding the Bravo vehicles home, and he looked for sure like he was going to bring more strife than benefit to the convoy. Sitting in the tiny cabin of extremely thick Perspex, the driver, wearing NVGs with very limited visibility, lurched the vehicle left and right as the convoy of fighting vehicles headed towards the base.

Chatter rippled through the commandos' comms, voicing concern that the driver was going to roll the Chubby into a ditch. If that happened, they would have to spend the next few hours, possibly days, trying to get the bloody thing back on its wheels.

Then a figure emerged from the darkness, a flash of luminescent green across the soldiers' optics. He ran towards the vehicle and leapt onto its back. Over their comms, the Australians heard terse instructions being given to the driver of the vehicle.

It was Cam's voice.

'That was so Cam,' says Jack Ducat, a man who would become one of Cam's closest friends. 'If you went to him and said, "Did anyone tell you to do that?" he would have said, "Nah." "Well, why'd you do it?" "Mate, we needed to get back." If an IED had gone off he would have been fucked, but we did need to get back so he just took action. That's just how he was – pragmatic. Part of the reason he was such a great soldier was because everything was so black and white for him.'

—

Back at TK the jobs continued apace. Most missions involved a vehicle drop some distance away from a target, a long walk, a short raid – perhaps involving

146

a firefight – intelligence and matériel gathering, and then a long walk back to the vehicles again.

This operational cadence would change in the coming rotations, but Rot Five was defined by long drives, long marches, many fruitless clearances, then marches and drives back to base. The most common questions in the pre-mission briefings were: 'How long is the walk going to be?' and 'How many aqueducts do we have to climb over?'

It was an exhausting tour. The boys from Bravo tried to keep their strength up, but with so much time outside the wire, and such long marches as part of each job, many reported losing 10 to 12 kilograms through the deployment.

Some soldiers fell sick, reporting flu-like symptoms or explosive diarrhoea. When someone presented with such symptoms, they were quarantined in one of the huts back in TK. Just before the defining mission of Rot Five, two of the team commanders were confined and unable to perform duties. One of them was Cam's team commander.

As a result, Cameron Baird stepped up and commanded the team. Time would prove that this was his calling.

The mission was a long vehicle interdiction in the Mirabad Valley, a poor, predominantly Pashtun area that was soon known to the Aussie soldiers as Mira-badass Valley, due to the increasing likelihood of attack there.

After getting to the valley, the commandos conducted a series of compound raids, each one adding to the intelligence picture and informing the next raid. One lunchtime the team commanders were told that a new target had emerged: the village of Chenartu. A number of Taliban were expected to be there, and possibly even the 'shadow governor' of the province, Mullah Baz Mohammad.

Shadow governors were not only responsible for fundraising and recruitment, they were also often top-tier field commanders, the men who planned attacks against coalition soldiers. Mullah Baz Mohammad would be quite the scalp.

There wasn't a lot of visual information on Chenartu village. The soldiers had some satellite imagery of the area, which had been sent to the vehicles, but it wasn't as detailed as they would have liked. Despite this, the team commanders started putting together a plan for an assault on 23 November 2007.

They would be attacking a series of linked buildings. The plan was to come into the village as one force, before pausing at a forming-up point (FUP) about a kilometre away from the closest building. An overwatch element would be left at the FUP, and the rest of the commandos would insert into the middle of the compounds. There they would split into two assault teams, 'King' and 'Lincoln', sweeping east and west, respectively. Cam was part of assault team Lincoln, as was Eddie.

The commandos got to the vehicle drop-off (VDO) area, which, due to unexpectedly difficult terrain, was quite a long distance from the compounds. The walk in would be a gruelling, steep and rocky 10 kilometres.

Each man remembers the cold, long slog down to the village, and many recall an even more concerning aspect of the traverse: the brightness of the sky. The assault teams started their way down to the compound at dusk, planning to attack under the cover of darkness, but the moon was high and full that night. While moving from high ground to low, Jack Ducat was concerned they would be spotted before the assault could begin.

'That walk was taking a while,' he says. 'It was a massive open field of nothing, and as we walked I just kept looking at the compounds sitting down there, thinking, *Fuck, they're going to bump* [see] *us for sure.*'

The soldiers got up to the FUP around 11 p.m. The team commanders crept to a bluff so they could eyeball the compounds they were to be attacking. They spotted two unarmed men walking along a path between the compounds and a creek. This was unusual: rarely did they see people walking around Afghan compounds so late at night. Ten minutes later, four more unarmed men passed along the path.

Bar the soft crunch of boots on ground, there had been no noise during the walk in, but then the large working dogs that are found in most Afghan compounds started barking. The team commanders were uneasy about the number of people around but didn't think they had been sprung, so they decided to push on with the assault. The two teams moved quietly and slowly towards their assault points.

As Richie 'Boy' Young, a commander in assault team King, moved along an alley, he sensed someone behind him. He turned and, in the shimmering green of NVG illumination, saw a figure only a few metres away. 'I'd just walked past there, so this guy must have come out of a doorway or something,' he says. 'It was the first time I'd seen the enemy up close. We'd been in plenty of contacts, but this was the first time I was pretty much face-to-face with one of them. He was the quintessential Taliban – black dishdash, *shemagh* [scarf] wrapped around his head, big black beard and AK.'

Young got the impression that the man had seen something but wasn't sure what. Young was facing away from the enemy fighter, so he started, very slowly, to turn his body and rifle around. 'I was thinking, *Fuck, he might have the drop on me here*,' he says.

Suddenly, the gunman recognised what was in front of him. He raised his weapon to fire but never got the chance to pull the trigger. One of Young's team had come out of another doorway and hit the Taliban fighter with two rounds. Young quickly closed the distance on the man and put two more rounds in him. The enemy fell dead.

Both the commandos had noise suppressors affixed to their rifles, but in the dead of night the sound of the shots travelled. As these shots were fired, Baird's team, Lincoln, were stacked up against a locked compound door, which they needed to breach before they could start their assault.

Protocols had changed in the lead-up to this raid: previously, explosive charges might have been used for this type of entry, but there had been pushback on these because of the toll they were taking on rural Afghan people's nerves and property. So for this entry crowbars were used, which was nowhere near as effective. The team were having trouble getting through the locked door.

'I don't remember how long it actually took, but it seemed to take forever,' says Eddie. 'All that banging was going on, and I was like, *Fuck, we really need to get into there now.*'

Eddie was the third member of the 'stack'. After gaining entry, he was supposed to move to a specific firing position, after Luke Worsley and Ian Harry had taken their positions. It was the kind of entry the boys had done a thousand times before, either in their TAG (East) work or as part of the Advanced Close Quarters Battle course that preceded deployment. The difference here was the time it was taking them to get inside.

Finally, the compound door swung open and, with their NVGs on and their rifles at the ready, the commandos moved towards their positions. Luke Worsley was the first man through the door. As soon as he was moving, he shouted a target indication: 'There's a man on the roof!'

The machine-gun fire came in immediately, with at least two enemy combatants shooting at the doorway. Bullets slammed into the wall, the door and Luke. Dust swirled around, visibility went down, the cacophonous crackle of 5.56 mm and 7.72 mm rounds bounced around the compound walls.

'[Later] I looked at the wall where the fire came in initially,' Eddie says, 'and I'm still stunned that only one of the blokes went down. The amount of fire that they had on us was really something.'

Ian Harry was pinned behind a column and Luke was on the ground. Eddie and Cam entered, returning fire and suppressing the Taliban guns. Cam ordered Eddie and Ian to pull Luke out of the compound. There, Cam told Eddie to make a medical assessment of the 26-year-old.

The brothers at their home in Upper Burnie, Tasmania. Cameron was not quite two and a half and Brendan was eight.

By the time he was seven, Cameron's athletic talent was more than apparent, and he had the trophies to prove it.

Cam had just won the gold medal for discus at the Diamond Valley Regional Championships. This is what you call a winning smile.

The Baird brothers, Cam (eight and a half) and Brendan (fourteen), sporting matching haircuts.

Christmas 1989: Cam showing off a prized catch during a Queensland holiday. He was eight and a half.

Cam's fifth-grade school photo from Gladstone Views Primary School. By the end of that year people started assuming he was destined for an AFL career.

When he wasn't playing footy or listening to AC/DC, Cam was messing around on motorbikes with Brendan, or hunting or fishing with Doug, Brendan and his grandfather.

Cam holding the Holden Premiers Cup with (*left to right*): Dan Carole, Rick Green and Russell Vidoni.

Cameron was the Captain of the Victorian Schoolboys AFL team and already focused on playing hard and winning. He was regularly one of the 'best on ground'.

Here he is with the Keith Greig Medal for winning the Essendon District Football League Competition's Under 16 Best & Fairest Award that year. He only played six games (the broken arm had something to do with that) but he still received six 'best on ground' to win the medal.

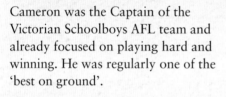

Year 12 Gladstone Park Secondary College. At the time this photo was taken, Cam believed he was on the right path to an AFL career.

Cam and his Uncle Ken used to have regular jam sessions. Music, including playing guitar, was one of Cam's great loves.

Cam's first game for the Geelong Reserves in July 1999. People fully expected that he would not only become an AFL player, but also a great.

Cameron Baird graduated from Kapooka on 18 February 2000, and at the March Out Parade he was named 'Most Outstanding Soldier' in his platoon.

Cam with his Grandad, John Baird, on March Out Day in Wagga Wagga.

At the end of infantry training, Cam joined the 4RAR Commando regiment. Commando training was a whole new level from what he'd experienced before. And it would cost him his two front teeth.

Cam moved to Holsworthy and immersed himself in army life (*left*). But then he met Robin and at 22, he married.

Brendan, Kaye, Cam and Doug on Cameron's wedding day.

Eddie turned on his light and looked at his compatriot. He had head wounds which were undoubtedly fatal.

'He's gone, mate,' Eddie reported to Cam.

'Epsilon is en route, mate,' Cam replied, citing the company medic's call sign. 'Stay here until handover, then I need you back in there.'

A man had died under Cameron Baird's command, but there was still a job to do, and other comrades to defend. The sound of gunfire was still ringing through the compound, as soldiers from both King and Lincoln teams were engaged.

The machine gun rattled again towards Cam's team, who were trapped near the doorway where Luke had been killed. The compound was a small one, perhaps no bigger than a basketball court, but it was a warren of rooms and doors around a courtyard. At one end Australian soldiers were pinned down; at the other was the roaring machine gun.

Cam saw a position in the middle of the courtyard where he could get defilade, or protection, from the machine gun. As his team covered him, he sprinted through the gunfire to the position. When he got there, fire from an AK-47 came from another direction, in front of him and on the second floor. Cam started hurling grenades at the new positions and at the machine gun, as well as putting rounds towards both.

'I was still trying to get my bearings when he ran in,' says Jason Turner, another of the commandos on the assault team. 'We all were. He was five or ten metres ahead of the rest of us, on his own, firing his weapon and tossing grenades. It was incredible. That machine gun could have killed all [of us].'

Soon the Taliban guns were suppressed and the Australians started moving forward. As they did, one of the soldiers saw a young Afghan boy walking around, dazed.

'It was difficult for the boys,' says Richie Young. 'They were being shot at but they knew that women and children were in there as well. They couldn't just start engaging, so they had to start moving around the compound without hurting the people who were being used as human shields.'

The soldiers started to go from room to room. In one, Cam found himself face-to-face with a Taliban fighter, his rifle pointed at the door.

'Old mate froze and Cam was at the ready, so that was that,' one of the soldiers in the assault says.

Jason Turner moved into the room from which the AK-47 fire had been coming. A figure lay dead, the gender unrecognisable because of the effects of the grenades. A report later mentioned at least one female combatant;

this may have been her. In the room Turner also found a baby, estimated to be six months old. It had been wrapped up in cloth, and one of the other soldiers almost stepped on the child until Turner realised what it was. The baby was obviously distressed. Turner lowered his rifle, scooped up the child and moved it out of the way.

When they got to the end of the compound, they found the PK (Pulemyot Kalashnikov) machine-gunner dead. The commandos entered the room below and found that it had been the 'women's room'. Often in these rural Afghan compounds, the women and girls slept in one room together; it was from above this room that the Taliban fighter had been machine-gunning the commandos.

Against the wall were a huddle of children, bunched on a mattress. They were crying but unhurt. Next to them was a woman who had been shot in the leg. A teenage girl was lying on the ground. She was dead. While the machine-gunner was being suppressed, a great deal of fire had entered this room also.

Eddie tried to administer medical treatment to the woman who had been shot, but she screamed every time he approached. Cam and Jason went back and checked the rooms again in reverse, making sure the compound had been completely cleared.

During the reverse clearance, they had only one surprise, but it was an awful one. The baby they had moved was now dead. The child had no external injuries, but had likely sustained fatal internal wounds from the concussion of grenades.

'You take fire from a room, you return fire and grenades go in, and sometimes the wrong people are killed. It really fucking sucks but it happens,' one of the commandos told me.

'That was a tough day,' says Richie Young. 'I know it really affected the boys.'

There was no time for Cam to reflect on what had happened. A drone above had found that there were other Taliban fighters converging on the village.

Twelve fighting-age men from the compound were handcuffed and ready for detention and tactical questioning, and King and Lincoln began 'site exploitation', or searches for evidence and documents. Cam and his team uncovered explosives, ammunition and bomb-making materials. They photographed the dead Taliban, their weapons still with them, and then they photographed the innocents who'd been killed in the crossfire. It was confirmed later that a number of the captured men were Taliban fighters, including one who had been preparing a suicide bomb attack. In line with Afghan custom, a payment was later arranged for the families of the civilian dead.

A casualty evacuation, or CASEVAC, was requested for Luke Worsley. The request was denied. At that point in the war, Australia had no dedicated air assets, and with other coalition battles happening concurrently, the Australian KIA (killed in action) had to wait. On later rotations some commandos would learn to call in their KIA as 'priority alpha' wounded, sometimes adding 'no vitals'.

The medic wrapped a *shemagh* around Luke's head and zip-tied his hands together. He was placed on a stretcher, and the assault teams were told that they needed to carry Luke out to the vehicle drop-off point.

'I could tell that the emotions were running high a little bit then, but we all snapped back in line pretty quickly,' Jack Ducat remembers. 'We're carrying him back out and that's it. Now the focus was back on security.'

The walk in to the compound from the vehicles had been long and tense, but the walk back was far worse. The commandos took turns in carrying the body of their dead friend, who weighed more than 100 kilograms. When they weren't carrying Luke, they had to look out for enemy fighters, who were still taking pot shots at the Australians. Bombs dropped from American drones from time to time as Taliban fighters tried to approach the returning commandos.

'That walk was easily the most arduous thing I've ever done, in my life,' says Richie Young.

No one spoke about Luke's death on the way back to the vehicles, nor as they waited for a helicopter to take him back to TK. Cam and Richie put his body in the back of a Bushmaster vehicle, zipping him up in a body bag. With dawn breaking, the pair kneeled silently next to their dead friend for a few moments before going back to their teams.

Back at his vehicle, Cam was told to get a few hours of kip, as new orders would be coming in soon. At 11 a.m. they were back in the cars, heading for a new objective. By dusk, they were ready for another night mission. For three more days Bravo conducted compound clearances in the Mirabad Valley.

—

Normally, when returning to Tarin Kowt after such a long job, the guys would feel a release, even joy, especially if the mission had been a success and enemy combatants had been killed. Not this time.

After resupplying the vehicles, each commando involved in the raid on Chenartu was called in for an after-action review. After explaining, in great detail, what their role had been that night, the commandos were told that Luke's ramp ceremony would take place the next day. Word spread around Bravo that there would be an earlier, informal send-off in the padre's sparse prayer hut.

Although Camp Russell was ostensibly a dry base, there were some supplies of beer in a Conex storage container, ready to be distributed sparingly by the cook on Christmas Day and Anzac Day. As the soldiers explained to me, the cook 'dropped his keys' that night. Beer flowed, music played and the exhausted soldiers of 4RAR got well and truly sideways.

'Dudes were emotive,' says Jack Ducat. 'They were upset and then a moment later jovial, telling stories. Everyone was a bit all over the place.'

A video taken that night shows soldiers exhibiting the unbridled energy that's released when dynamic youthfulness collides with the menace of death. It's the energy of heavy metal music, or gangster rap. In large groups the commandos shouted and joked and swore at each other. In smaller groups they talked about their homes and their partners.

'Truth is, the guys were vulnerable,' Richie Young recalls. 'A lot of us were thinking for a moment about our lives back home. Some of the guys started talking about their kids and how much they were looking forward to seeing them again. I remember Cam getting quite emotional that night. He told me he really wanted to have kids, and I remember saying, "It's all good, mate. You'll be a dad one day." That was one of the few times I ever saw him vulnerable.'

Dire Straits' 'Brothers in Arms' played on the portable speakers. As it did, Willy Lacquer realised that this rotation was going to be a life-defining event. These men around him would forever be his brothers, due to the bond forged in combat and the closeness of death.

Whatever else happened in these men's lives, there would be no escaping the memory of the last few days. They had all known that death was a part of the job, but previously it had been an abstract concept. Now they had seen its face.

The emotion of the night funnelled into a singular moment, which every man recalls. Cam Baird grabbed his guitar and, standing atop a table, told the babbling crowd to shut the fuck up. Then he started strumming a familiar tune: the opening chords to American pop-punk trio Green Day's 'Good Riddance (Time of Your Life)'.

Cam sang with his head down and his eyes closed, dedicating himself to the moment. The other soldiers either joined in or were silent.

As so often appears the case in a time of extreme emotional stress and revelation, the song's lyrics seemed to speak truly to the men. This moment was a turning point for the young soldiers. Time and circumstance had grabbed them by the wrist and dragged them into territory that few Australians in the twenty-first century had travelled to. It was a place they'd wanted to visit, and now they knew it was a place that one did not just visit. They would not return from this rotation unaffected, for better or worse. This was not a question but a lesson. Cam sang that he hoped that they had the time of their lives.

Every man in that room had gone through infantry training. Every man had gone through commando training. Every man had said he wanted to be in combat. Every man had now seen the mad, random, violent nakedness of war. Most in the room wanted more combat, but some did not. After that rotation, a few requested transfers to a regular unit. No one judged them; combat wasn't for everybody.

Combat was for Cameron Baird. He later told his brother that Afghanistan had been exactly what he'd expected, and exactly what he'd wanted. He had thought previously that he was a commando; now he knew he was. Cam also told his brother that he still had so much to do to become the commando he wanted to be.

The next day, Luke Worsley left Afghanistan. A bearer party of commandos carried a coffin draped in an Australian flag, with Luke's green beret atop it. Slowly they moved to an Australian C-130 transport, with an honour guard of Australian, American, Dutch and Afghan soldiers flanking them.

After Luke's body was sent home, operations continued for Bravo until, as the days became colder and shorter, the fighting season came to an end. One of Bravo's platoons was sent home before Christmas. A few weeks after that, Cam's platoon followed, arriving in Sydney on Australia Day 2008.

Upon touching down, Cam travelled to the suburb of Windsor to give his commiserations to Luke's parents, John and Marjorie Worsley. He told them that Luke's last words had been a target indication, a warning for his mates. Luke had served and fought till his last breath.

Cam would continue visiting Luke Worsley's parents until he, too, was killed in action while trying to protect his brothers.

CHAPTER NINE

GALLANTRY

'I told [Cameron] I thought he was taking
too much of the burden, but, you know,
that is the nature of leadership.'

MAJOR JACK THURGAR

GALLIPOLI, TURKEY
SYDNEY, NEW SOUTH WALES
2008–09

There were two official inquiries into the raid in Chenartu,
one investigating the circumstances of Luke Worsley's death
and the other investigating potential collateral damage
issues, including the civilian deaths. Both found that all
deaths, on the Afghan side and on the Australian side,

were a regrettable but normal side-effect of the kind of operations the Australians were undertaking. In short, the intelligence was good, the equipment was good, the command structure was good, the procedures and execution were good, but it was simply in the nature of war that people were sometimes killed.

The second investigation, moreover, found that not only were the commandos not at fault, they likely saved some lives with their decisive action. Of the commandos, the report noted:

> There is overwhelming suggestion that control was being exerted and their actions were well coordinated. It is the assessment of the IO [investigating officer] that given the closeness and intensity of the fighting within such a complex environment, additional casualties, both friendly and non-combatant, would most likely have resulted had effective control and coordination not been present.

After Rot Five, the Army was looking for junior leaders in each branch of the Australian military for a new initiative called 'I'm an Australian Soldier'. In the program, 15 defence personnel – one from each individual command – would help promote nine values across the armed forces, including toughness, leadership, initiative and compassion.

The soldiers were chosen not only because they represented the values identified, but also because of their ability to disseminate those values to the soldiers above and below their pay grade.

Cameron Baird was the junior leader chosen from the Special Operations Command.

The program was to culminate in a journey to Gallipoli, Turkey, where the 15 soldiers would, on Anzac Day, speak to the international visitors who had travelled to Lone Pine. Beforehand, they were to travel to Canberra to study the Gallipoli campaign in great detail, from the strategy and weaponry to the personalities and emotions of the Diggers.

The man coordinating the program was an SAS major named John 'Jack' Thurgar, who had, like Major Fleer, been one of the 'phantoms of the jungle' in Vietnam and had a great deal of special-operations combat experience. Major Thurgar became fast friends with Cam, who came to see him as a mentor. In Canberra they studied together and prepared for the trip to Turkey, but they also talked about Cam's recent combat experiences.

The death of Luke Worsley weighed heavily on Cam's mind. Although his actions in Chenartu had been exceptional, Cam felt that he needed more training – that perhaps he had been underprepared. Thurgar told Cam about Sir John Monash, one of the Australian commanders in Gallipoli, whose experiences in the stalled Dardanelles campaign pushed him both personally and professionally.

'Monash thought, *I have to do this better. I have to get a new level of professionalism*,' says Thurgar. 'It happens to all of us. We all have to do better when we're soldiers in a time of war. I told [Cameron] I thought he was taking too much of the burden, but, you know, that is the nature of leadership.'

Also on Cam's mind were the civilian deaths in Chenartu. He and Thurgar spoke about what had happened, but the contents of that conversation remain private. For soldiers, there are some topics that can only be discussed with other soldiers.

During their time together in Canberra, Thurgar says, he developed an immense appreciation for his young charge. Not only was Cam a quick and diligent study on military affairs – in stark contrast to his time in high school – Thurgar was also impressed by his character and demeanour.

'He was just honest and reliable and trustworthy,' he says. 'All the qualities you'd want in a soldier and a best mate. I got a sense that he'd always stand up for his blokes, and if he thought you were being a dickhead and that was going to affect his guys, even if you were an officer, you were going to know it.'

Cam had already developed an appreciation for military history, but after this stint in Canberra it increased. After studying Gallipoli, he went back further in time, learning about the Scottish highland warriors, Julius Caesar and – a personal favourite – the Spartans.

A particularly militarist state, Sparta revered military service above all else, with training starting virtually at birth. A tombstone was reserved only for those who had died in combat during a victorious campaign. Spartan soldiers were also strict adherents to a code of honour and discipline, and were famous for living ascetically while on campaign.

This reflected Cam's own attitude when on deployment in Afghanistan. At Camp Russell, most Aussie soldiers chose to decorate their bunks with touches of home: pictures of loved ones, trinkets or other heirlooms. Not Cam. His bunk could always be easily identified: it would be made up, unadorned and with a packed bag under it at all times. Cam reasoned that if he were killed, it would be someone's job to go and pick up any pictures and knick-knacks he had about his bunk. Likely one of his mates. Cam didn't want anyone to have to do that. Not only was it an upsetting duty, it could affect that bloke when he was next outside the wire. For Cam, it was a question of mission readiness.

Cam's trip to Turkey was his first overseas journey without a gun. There, he could play the role that most young Australians enjoy taking on when travelling for the first time: that of the wide-eyed neophyte.

The 15 soldiers were billeted with Turkish families, and Cam enjoyed learning about moderate Islam from his hosts. In Afghanistan he had interacted with perhaps the most religiously conservative people on Earth, and, according to Jack Thurgar, he'd retained some anger towards the religion after Luke Worsley's death. Now that anger began to dissipate.

'The Turks are good people and Cam enjoyed their company,' Major Thurgar says. 'I believe I could see some calming happening while we were there.'

On Anzac Day, Cam spoke at Lone Pine, a location where Australian forces attacked Ottoman trenches as part of the August Campaign, the British attempt to take the Gallipoli Peninsula. The Australian push was successful, but part of a losing campaign.

Cam read an excerpt from the diary of Ion Idriess, a notable and prolific Australian author who fought at Gallipoli and later wrote a series of military handbooks called *The Australian Guerrilla*, many of which are about early special-operations tactics.

At Gallipoli, Jack Thurgar tried to get his young charges into the minds of the soldiers who fought in the campaign there. He arranged for the soldiers to paddle in kayaks, pre-dawn, to Anzac Cove, just as the Diggers had in 1915. He made for them the bully beef stew that was eaten so many years ago in the Dardanelles. Together they walked through the graves of the war dead.

Many Australians have travelled to Turkey and spent time imagining what battle must be like. Cam didn't have to imagine. Back in Sydney, thoughts of battle were rarely from his mind. For every commando, the mountains of Afghanistan always loom on the horizon. Now Cam had an even greater desire to be as close to a perfect soldier as possible.

—

Between trips to Afghanistan, Bravo Company was taking on a contingency role. This meant they were training in forests and waterways, ready to defend northern Australia or deploy again to East Timor, as one of the companies had in 2006, when a coup threatened the young nation.

While Cam was training in this contingency role, a decision was made to consider him for a battlefield honour after the raid in Chenartu. For a soldier to be considered for such an award, an officer has to submit a document explaining why the operator under their command met the criteria for a specific award. It was decided that Cam should be nominated for the Medal for Gallantry, the third-highest award in the Australian military honours system, awarded for 'acts of gallantry in hazardous circumstances'.

The first Cam knew about it was when a letter arrived.

Dear Lance Corporal Baird,

I am writing on behalf of the Governor-General to inform you that you are being considered for the award of the Medal for Gallantry within the Australian Honours System.

It went on to say that if Cam agreed to accept the award, he should sign and return the enclosed form and privacy agreement. Cam showed the letter to his brother one day when they were sitting in the back of their parents' car.

Brendan was blown away. 'That's awesome, mate,' he said.

Cam didn't think so. He didn't feel that what he'd done in Chenartu was exceptional. He thought that every man had done his job, including him. As far as Cam was concerned, there was no reason to highlight his role and not that of the others.

'I reckon I'm gonna turn it down,' he told his brother.

Brendan didn't understand, but the guys back at Holsworthy did. They knew Cam wasn't the kind of bloke who liked to be singled out. Standing up there on stage and having medals pinned on him by politicians was not why Cam was in the Army. It certainly wasn't why he was a commando.

Cam wanted to do the job because it was difficult. And when it was difficult, he didn't want to be rewarded for doing it – this was what he'd wanted all along. It's also possible that his reluctance may have stemmed from the fact that there were civilian casualties in Chenartu, too.

His mates in Bravo Company pushed him to accept the award. There had been six MGs awarded in Afghanistan to that point, and five of them had gone to the SASR boys from Perth. It was time for the tempo and intensity of the work that 4RAR was doing to be recognised too. 'Take it for the commandos, Cam,' they said. 'Take it for Bravo.'

That argument spoke to Cam. He didn't buy into the Perth–Sydney tensions, but he was incredibly proud of what his unit was becoming. Cam sent back the forms.

A few months later, another letter arrived, telling him to report to Admiralty House in Sydney for the ceremony. Cam's guests were Doug, Kaye and Robin. Cam's parents flew to Sydney and met Robin and Cam at their place near

Holsworthy, and then they all packed into Cam's tiny red Mazda 121 for the drive to the city.

Cam's invitation indicated that he had two sartorial options: his polyester dress uniform (known as 'polys') or a suit. At such ceremonies the Army expects soldiers to choose the former, but Cam opted for the latter: a dark suit, shirt and tie. Cam hated those polys. In most military forces there are soldiers who relish marching, saluting and wearing polys, and others who preferred getting cammed up, gunned up and in the face of the enemy. Cam was the latter type of soldier.

The other sartorial choice Cam had made was a pair of black wraparound prescription sunglasses, which had some black electrical tape on one side to keep the arm from falling off. He kept these on as the invitees and guests milled around before the official proceedings began. He had regular glasses but had left them at home.

'Some pompous protocol peanut had some issue with them,' Jack Ducat remembers. 'Cam's so blunt, so black and white. The bloke asked Cam why he was wearing them and he said, "Mate, I can't see. They're prescription."'

The ceremony was a dour one, with the only moment of levity coming when Cam stepped onto the stage and gave a rock sign, to the amusement of Jack Ducat, who was there as the guest of another soldier, and Cam's family.

'Cam did like to let the air out of the balloon,' Doug says.

For Cam, the medal was not for him but for all in Bravo Company. It was recognition of how far the unit had come in a short time. But what really mattered to Cam was getting back into the action. And that wasn't far away.

As the soldiers got closer to their second Afghan deployment, the tempo of training changed, not quickening, as you might expect, but slowing, with the soldiers fearing an injury that might keep them from taking that brown route trip back to Tarin Kowt.

As the deployment date approached, Afghanistan went from being in the back of the soldiers' minds to the front. Every man remembered his recent combat, thinking about what they would do differently the next time. Excitement was building. This time they would do everything better.

Before the commandos had even left Australia, news started to filter through that they had been assigned their first mission, and it was going to be a big one. They would be going further south, in an operation that would undoubtedly mean a shitload of combat.

Bravo was going to Helmand.

CHAPTER TEN

THE KAJAKI DIVERSION

*'Sun would be shining, AC/DC would be blasting
and these big dudes with their shirts off would be
loading massive amounts of ammunition on the cars
for a huge mission. They were happy as shit.'*

RICHIE YOUNG

HELMAND PROVINCE, AFGHANISTAN
2009

In Afghanistan in 2008, COIN was the word. The
'COINdanistas', as the proponents of COIN had been
dubbed, had taken charge of the direction of the war. If
you were an officer in Afghanistan above a certain pay
grade, you were probably saying the word 'COIN' a lot.

A portmanteau of the words 'counter' and 'insurgency', COIN denoted a set of evolving strategies developed by top military thinkers, the most recent being the Australian academic Dr David Kilcullen, who co-wrote the US Army's field manual on counter-insurgency, and General David Petraeus, who had both redefined and (supposedly) proven the latest COIN theories while serving in Iraq.

COIN essentially dictated that if you wanted to defeat an insurgency, you first had to defeat their ideas. You had to prove to the civilian population that life would be better for them if you prevailed, rather than your insurgent enemy – in this case, the Taliban.

With that in mind, the coalition green-lit a series of large reconstruction projects in 2008. Perhaps none was more ambitious than the refurbishment of the Kajaki Dam, in Helmand Province.

The dam had been constructed in the 1950s by the United States Agency for International Development (USAID), a government organisation that helped third-world countries with infrastructure projects – especially those countries that were in danger of becoming second-world, or communist, countries.

After a couple of decades as an irrigation dam, Kajaki became a source of hydroelectric power after USAID fitted it with two turbines. There were plans to raise the dam's height and install a third turbine, which would increase the dam's power output by almost 100 per cent, but then Afghanistan was invaded by the Soviet Union. For 30 years the country was at almost constant war; the dam was maintained but never upgraded. It continued producing the same kilowattage until, in October 2001, the US Air Force dropped a number of bombs on the dam. At that point it stopped producing power altogether.

From 2001, Kandahar, the nation's second-largest city, went through a series of rolling blackouts. In the aftermath, a common refrain could be heard: 'I was no fan of the dictatorship, but at least they kept the lights on.' To fulfil the power needs of the city, huge amounts of diesel had to be flown in, and even after the two turbines came back online – one in 2005 and the other in 2006 – the people still had to use massive quantities of solid fuels.

With a power crisis looming, USAID developed a plan to install the third turbine at Kajaki. Procuring it was easy, but much more difficult was convincing the military commands in Afghanistan to dedicate the resources required to delivering the new turbine to the dam. Time after time, requests to move the turbine were refused by military command until, in 2008 – and with the COINdanistas in the ascendancy – it was finally approved.

Soon afterwards, the British military (which was in charge of the area the dam was in) started planning what would be its biggest logistical mission since World War II.

The turbine was flown, in parts, to Kandahar airport in September 2008. The parts were then loaded onto more than 100 giant low-loader trucks, and the slow journey to Kajaki began. It was only 160 kilometres from the airport to the dam, but the journey was through some of the most dangerous territory in the country. More than 5000 soldiers, mostly British but also American and Australian, were tasked with providing security for the convoy, alongside attack helicopters, ground assault planes and drones. A dummy convoy of 40 trucks was also sent out of Kandahar by the Dutch Army, to confuse the Taliban.

When the turbine parts arrived safely at the dam, it seemed the mission had been a success. Taliban efforts to attack the convoy had been less concerted than expected, and they'd been repelled relatively easily. An estimated 250 Taliban had been killed during the operation, but only one coalition soldier had died, hitting an IED on his way back to his base.

In a moment of perhaps reckless optimism, Brigadier Mark Carleton-Smith, the British officer in charge of the operation, spoke to the press after the mission and claimed that the Taliban 'no longer enjoy popular consent from the

Afghan people, who are overwhelmingly hostile to them. Clearly they no longer represent to that extent a strategic threat to the government.' The achievement was presented as a huge COIN win.

But was it? Moving the turbine to the dam didn't mean much to the Afghan people unless it began generating the power that went to their homes, and it turned out that was still a long way away. Even with the turbine at the dam, there was much to do to get it working. Installation equipment was needed, not to mention the hundreds of tonnes of cement required to set the turbine in place. There was also the question of the huge infrastructure upgrade that was needed to get the power from the dam to Kandahar.

In fact, the operation had so far produced a negative COIN effect. An entire division of coalition soldiers had been repurposed for the mission, and while they were planning and executing the convoy, the Taliban had made major territorial gains in the places from which the soldiers had been diverted. There was a huge list of tasks that still had to be completed before any COIN benefit could be reaped, but reassigning another division was impossible. These tasks would have to be checked off slowly, while a large contingent of soldiers protected the dam and surrounds.

By the time Bravo arrived in Afghanistan for their next rotation, this protective effort was taking a toll on the British military. The dam had been guarded by British paratroopers, but the constant harassment to which they'd been exposed had been taxing. They were to be relieved by US Marines but, like everything to do with Kajaki, this would be a logistical nightmare, and during the changeover period the dam would be prone to attack.

A plan was developed. While the Americans were replacing the British, two coalition special forces groups would be sent into the Kajaki 'Fan', the plain north of the dam, where many of the Taliban in Helmand lived and operated. The special forces would present for battle, hunt Taliban commanders and generally keep the bad guys so busy that they wouldn't even know about the changeover.

The two special forces groups chosen for the job were an element of US Army Green Berets and Bravo Company, who had just arrived back at TK. It would be the first job for the commandos as they started Rot Nine.

—

As soon as Cameron Baird reached Camp Russell he started his mission prep, of which there was quite a lot. But he couldn't wait to get out on this Kajaki job. He'd developed a taste for battle.

This was the first time Australian commandos were going to be in Helmand, perhaps Afghanistan's most violent province. The first time in earnest, anyway. One of the other commando companies had made a minor incursion into Helmand before, but that had been nothing like this promised to be. This mission was planned to go for weeks, and for most of them Bravo was going to be out looking for fights.

It had been stressed to the soldiers beforehand that there would doubtless be casualties on this trip. Every soldier in the company was obliged to make out a will and write a death note to his loved ones. Many of the guys just put an empty sheet of paper into an envelope.

It was an order, though, so it's possible Cam penned a few perfunctory lines. Like others, though, he thought having to write a note like this was bad luck. He resented the task, much as he resented having to pose, clean-shaven and in his polys, for a photograph that would be used in the event he was killed.

For this mission, Cam would once again be a vehicle commander and 2IC of his team. Working with Cam and his vehicle would be Mervyn 'Merv' McDonald, who some said was so like Cam you could mistake them for brothers, and Timmy 'Aps' Aplin, who at 37 was a few years older than the others; he'd relinquished a higher rank so he could move from a regular unit into the special forces. All three were big, burly blokes who loved heavy metal music, taking the piss out of each other and relentless, forward-foot fighting. They got along like a house on fire, and to a man could not have been more excited about the prospect of heading into the Taliban heartland.

Richie Young vividly remembers walking past Cam Baird's vehicle bay and sensing his excitement. 'Sun would be shining, AC/DC would be blasting and these big dudes with their shirts off would be loading massive amounts of ammunition on the cars for a huge mission,' he says. 'They were happy as shit.'

The mission started in March 2009, with the Australian convoy driving east to Firebase Tycz, an American outpost where Bravo would liaise with the Green Berets about how the Australian and American elements were to operate in the Fan. Afterwards, they set off south towards the dam, and almost straightaway encountered a field of improvised explosive devices.

This was IED country. Huge, rocky high ground and scarce passes defined this part of Afghanistan, and once the Taliban saw the general direction of the coalition convoys, it was easy for them to presume the route. When they found a chokepoint, they'd pack it with IEDs.

Bravo was travelling with six engineers from the Incident Response Regiment (IRR), and when the convoy hit such a chokepoint, the vehicles would stop and the IRR element would move forward to sweep for mines.

Just out of Tycz, in a place called the Chamberak Valley, the IRR found 19 IEDs in a 1-kilometre stretch of road. Almost all were homemade bombs attached to pressure plates, waiting for the wheels of the Australian vehicles. Eighteen of the IEDs were destroyed in controlled detonations. One was not.

As the IRR worked, one of the commandos in each vehicle would man his vehicle's fixed gun, scanning for attackers, while the other two slept, read or watched films on their iPhones. Sometimes a call would come over the comms saying that an IED had been found. Then came a countdown before a controlled detonation.

4 ... 3 ... 2 ... 1 ... BOOM.

Afterwards, the drivers might be told to move up a few metres. If one of the soldiers needed to go to the toilet, they'd do it off the back of the vehicles. If they wanted to eat, they had their MREs. The hours were long and slow for the commandos, in great contrast to the immensely tough, dangerous and tiring work the IRR boys were doing around the clock.

By the end of the first day the IRR team was exhausted, but they had to keep working through the night. At the start of the second day, a little after dawn on 19 March 2009, an IED detection call came over the radio, then the countdown, then a detonation. A couple of minutes later there was another detonation – this time much louder.

'I remember the second explosion going off and thinking, *They didn't call that over the radio*,' says Richie Young. 'I saw a bunch of sandbags flying up, but they weren't sandbags, it was Brett.'

Sergeant Brett Till, the 31-year-old father of two who had been commanding the IRR element, had been blown up. Till had identified a 20-kilogram IED, and then had detonated a controlled charge. Afterwards, he wasn't sure that the IED had been destroyed so went in to inspect it. It detonated as he stood over it. It's not known how the IED exploded, but it's possible a second trigger was attached to the bomb – possibly a mercury switch, which sets the bomb off when it's no longer lying flat.

After the explosion a call came over the radio, almost immediately: 'One friendly KIA. Stay put.'

For the next few hours the commandos remained mostly silent in their vehicles as the five men in the IRR team cleared the ground. The IRR also had to search for Brett Till's 'mission-critical' gear: his armour, radios and weapons. Having collected Brett's body and his gear, his mates then had to continue clearing the path, ensuring their minds, bodies and souls were fully committed to the job at hand.

It took the convoy two full days to get through the IED field, and the IRR techs had worked around the clock. They went down through a pass, and then up through a pass, at a snail's pace, until finally the convoy made it to the Fan.

It had been a taxing time, and Cam and the rest of the Bravo team were very happy to stop, get out of their vehicles and cook some hot food. As they did, they watched the IRR soldiers move around them like ghosts, looking for somewhere they could rest their bodies, and gather their thoughts and their nerves.

'You could tell by looking at them that they were all just broken,' says Santiago 'Santi' Sambara, a junior soldier on his first rotation. 'They're such a small, tight-knit group. They were working fucking hard and had just seen their leader killed.'

Richie Young, who was in a different car from Cam, thought this break in action would be a good opportunity to catch up with his mate. 'I remember I found this little patch of grass and called [Cam] over,' he says. 'We sit down, open up a ration pack and literally as soon as we started to talk ... *FZZZZZZZ* ... 107 rockets started flying in.'

The Taliban had been watching the Australians, and attacked as soon as they stopped to rest. The convoy took cover and waited for a follow-up attack, but it wasn't forthcoming. Later an American Black Hawk came in, picked up Brett Till's body and dropped off another explosive ordnance-detection technician. For the IRR there was still a shitload of work to do, and no time to grieve.

As the convoy moved south, the team would sometimes conduct night raids on villages when there was intelligence that Taliban targets were likely to be found there. For many of the commandos on their first special-operations deployment, these engagements were their first direct-action missions. Sneaking into compounds bathed in green light, both officers and enlisted men looked to those fighters who had already raided in Afghanistan for guidance. Many looked to Cam.

More than anything else, Cam believed in the importance of initiative, decision and overwhelming intention. On one of the first raids into a village during the Kajaki job, the assault force took a couple of ineffective shots from a nearby hill. Everyone took cover, including the platoon commander, who was one of the first-timers.

'We got shot at, but there was nothing in it,' says Santi. 'Just a few shots from a goat herder or something. All the new guys hunkered down, including the platoon HQ, and they didn't want to move. Cam was telling them it was all fine, but they didn't believe him until he walked into an alleyway with his arms out, as though he was waiting for rain.'

Only then did the assault force emerge and continue the clearance.

Rain did come shortly after, bucketing down and filling the open-topped patrol vehicles with water. Before setting out on the mission, Jack Ducat had asked Cam what personal items he was taking with him. Cam made sure that he had speakers for the vehicle, but he wasn't taking much more.

'You're not taking Gore-Tex?' Ducat asked, referring to his waterproof wet-weather gear.

'Nah, it doesn't rain in Afghanistan,' Cam replied.

Ducat smiles as he remembers seeing Cam sitting in his vehicle and being lashed with rain, trying to squeeze his large body into small plastic bags in an attempt to stay dry. 'We'd been doing it pretty tough,' he says, 'but seeing Cam stuffed into a garbage bag just hating life was an instant morale booster.'

Cam wasn't the only one having a few issues with the weather. Many of the vehicles broke down, forcing the convoy to move off the low ground and into the mountains, where they set up an ad hoc garage. After a security cordon was established, vehicle pits were dug so the mechanics could access the car undercarriages. A list of parts needed was sent to HQ, and eventually some Chinooks arrived with axles, gearboxes and differentials. With the parts fitted, the group continued towards the Kajaki Fan.

It had been estimated that the Australian force would get to the middle of the Fan in three days, but it had taken almost two weeks. Now they were spoiling for a fight. So too were the Taliban.

—

One of the defining characteristics of the fighting in Uruzgan was the Afghans' propensity for shooting at the Australians and then dropping their weapons and running away. The Australian rules of engagement dictated how and when Australian soldiers were permitted to kill, and over time the Taliban came to understand how those rules were applied in the field.

In Helmand, however, the Taliban were more inclined to stay in the fight. On the radios the Afghan fighters called themselves 'the real mujahedin', the men who had seen off the Soviets and the Najibullah and Rabbani governments, and would now see off ISAF.

In the huge, flat expanse of the Fan, it was almost impossible for the Taliban to ambush the Australian force. The Taliban often knew exactly where the commandos were and where they were going, though, so the result was that the fighting was often more conventional than the commandos had become used to.

The commandos would set themselves up outside the effective range of small-arms fire and RPGs, only having to send patrols out looking for the 107 mm rocket launchers, the 82 mm mortars and the recoilless rifles that the Taliban in that area used, many of which were attached to battered old Toyota Hiluxes.

From their camps in the plains, the commandos would roll out into the Fan's villages, challenging the Taliban who were there to fight, which they did, seemingly out of habit.

'It was awesome fighting, real gentlemen's hours,' says Ian Turner. 'We'd line up our vehicles [in front of a village] in the morning and wait. Eventually a rocket would come in and it was fucking on. Later in the afternoon the shooting would stop, we'd pull back, get some food in, get some kip, have brekkie and start all over again.'

In these battles the commandos had a huge technical advantage, and would often outrange the Taliban, but otherwise they were still subject to the tools of asymmetric warfare used by a seasoned insurgent force.

On a night patrol on 3 April 2009, the target was a village called Sultan Rabat. Some vehicles were sent to high ground to cover the force below. As they moved along, the fifth vehicle in the line was launched into the sky after hitting a double-stacked anti-tank mine. Two of the men inside the vehicle were thrown out, landing many metres from the wrecked LRPV. They suffered only minor wounds. The driver, Damien Thomlinson, bore most of the kinetic energy of the blast, which caused horrendous injuries, pulping his legs and shattering his arms.

Thomlinson's life was saved by the men on the ground, and especially his mate Ian Turner. They pinched his femoral arteries to stop the bleeding, cleared his airways and stabilised him for a tense and bloody hour in enemy territory until a chopper arrived to get him to a base. Two days later, Thomlinson was in hospital in Germany.

The realities of war were impossible to ignore. From the deaths and injuries the men had witnessed to the constant threat of minefields, the confrontations in the villages, the bombs dropped from planes and drones and the Taliban constantly trying to approach the Australians, every day in the Fan brought action. Australian commanders were working overtime.

So too were the Taliban commanders – and deliberately so. Part of the plan was to give them so much work that their chatter on their communication systems would be raised above the 'detection threshold'. Then the leaders could be identified and possibly targeted by the night assault teams.

The tempo of the fighting in the Fan was exhausting, but apparently not too much for the blokes in the car that had been dubbed 'Iron Maiden' – and especially not for its commander, Cam Baird.

'Bairdy just never slowed down, never was flustered,' says Richie Young. 'I've got this great footage – we're in a massive fight, and out of nowhere Cam comes across to have a convo. Shit's going everywhere, and he strolls over and he's like, "Hey, mate, what you wanna do next?" As though we're just out for a beer.'

Not only was Cam indefatigable when fighting, his enthusiasm for it never waned either.

'I remember being on the approach to a village, and then everything kicked off,' says Santi Sambara. 'All kinds of rounds coming in, and straightaway Cam jumped off the car and started shooting the 84 [an M3 Carl Gustaf rocket launcher]. He fired a round, then dropped the gun and fell into the dirt. I was like, "Oh, shit, he's been shot," but he popped up, did a pirouette and motioned to his ears. He'd fired a ridiculously loud system with no ear protection. We all had a giggle about it. Bullets were coming and we were back to fighting.'

After weeks of relentless fighting, most of the soldiers were exhausted and in desperate need of a resupply. They met up with the US Green Berets who had been fighting on the other side of the Fan and started to follow them as they retraced their north-eastern route to Firebase Tycz.

Deep in the mountains, they found that the Australian Bushmaster vehicles, which had a wider profile than the US Humvees, couldn't get around some of the tight passes, so a number of times they had to stop and set Bangalore torpedos and C4 charges to widen the path.

When they had a relatively open road ahead, the Green Berets and commandos still faced many long days of mine clearance. Then one of the Afghan National Army Hilux drivers offered, for a pile of American greenbacks, to 'trailblaze' in front of them. As long as the Humvees, Bushmasters and LRPVs stayed in his wheel tracks, they wouldn't set off any IEDs.

The Australians and the Americans both had patrol funds, so they agreed. In the cars the Australians speculated whether this guy knew something about this area that they didn't. In any event, they made it to the firebase safely.

The Australians, including the IRR guys, got a much-needed break on the route back from Tycz to Tarin Kowt. As they left the American base they were overtaken by an Afghan water truck. They stopped the driver and asked him where he was going, and it turned out he was going to TK. So the Australians got another trailblazer, and this time for free.

When they got back to TK they'd been in the field for almost a month. Most of the men in each car had become exceptionally tight, living, sleeping, eating, driving and fighting in close proximity to one another. Cam, Merv and Aps decided that, when they got back to Sydney, they'd have an 'Iron Maiden' reunion – and what better occasion than an AC/DC concert? For much of the time they'd spent in that car, it had been filled with the music of Bon, Brian and the Young brothers.

Tickets to the Australian leg of AC/DC's Black Ice tour went on sale shortly after the end of the Kajaki job. With the tour selling out in record time, it's likely that either Cam, Aps or Merv got online in the very early hours of the morning to purchase tickets. Somehow they managed to score them.

In July 2009 Cam flew back to Sydney, his second tour of Afghanistan over. A month before, on 19 June, 4RAR had been renamed as 2nd Commando Regiment.

In February 2010 the 'Iron Maiden' trio of Cam, Aps and Merv went to the AC/DC concert together. A few weeks later, Private Timothy Aplin, who had only one rotation under his belt, redeployed to Afghanistan, having moved from Bravo Company to Alpha Company so he could get more combat experience.

Aps fought in the Shah Wali Kot Offensive, one of the biggest engagements the Australian SOTG had in Afghanistan. At the end of that battle, on 21 June 2010, he and two other Sydney-based 2 Commando soldiers, Private Benjamin Chuck and Private Scott Palmer, were killed when a US Black Hawk crashed at night. Seven other Aussie commandos flying in the chopper were seriously wounded. It was one of the darkest days for the unit. But there were more dark days to come.

On 30 August 2012, 30-year-old Lance Corporal Mervyn McDonald was killed in Helmand, once again in a helicopter crash. Also killed in the crash was 23-year-old commando Private Nathanael 'Nate' Galagher, who many have said looked up to Merv in the same way Merv looked up to Cam.

As for the Kajaki Dam, many installation dates have come and gone in the nine years since the third turbine was delivered from Kandahar airport. The cement never arrived, though, and the grid linking the dam to the major population centres is still either substandard or non-existent.

The immense price of blood, lives and money paid while trying to upgrade the dam is now likely all for nothing. Not only is it all but impossible these days to move the large amounts of installation materials required from Kandahar to Kajaki, the dam may fall under Taliban control anyway.

The third turbine still lies in parts inside the dam, a slowly rusting monument to the broken hopes of COIN, and a reminder of how much easier it is to destroy than to build in Afghanistan.

CHAPTER ELEVEN

COMMAND

'He was just born to lead.'

RICHIE YOUNG

TARIN KOWT, AFGHANISTAN
2009

Shortly after Bravo arrived back at Tarin Kowt from the Kajaki job, General Stanley McChrystal, now one of the most notable names in American special forces history, flew into Kabul to take command of ISAF.

The previous ISAF commander, General David McKiernan, had been relieved of his command by President Barack Obama, becoming the first American general to have been so dismissed in a time of war in 50 years. The European partners of ISAF were abandoning Afghanistan, and the Taliban were becoming more and more powerful. As a career special forces officer, McChrystal was an almost complete unknown to the American public and an unusual choice, but in this time of moderate crisis, and with special forces becoming an increasingly crucial part of all American operations overseas, his elevation seemed to make sense.

For five years McChrystal had been working across both Middle Eastern theatres of war as the commander of the United States' Joint Special Operations Command (JSOC), and in that time he'd had some very large wins. This included the capture of Saddam Hussein and the killing of hundreds of al-Qaeda operatives in Iraq, including that organisation's leader, Abu Musab al-Zarqawi. The killing of al-Zarqawi was a point of particular pride for the general, and he'd personally flown in after the air strike to identify the body.

During his tenure at JSOC, McChrystal was credited with modernising and revitalising the command. Although much of what JSOC did with McChrystal as its head is classified, it's known that, while the 2007 troop surge in Iraq was taking place, JSOC spooled up many operations in concert with the CIA to kill or capture hundreds of men suspected of being associated with al-Qaeda in Iraq.

At the time, those operations were deemed to have been an unmitigated success, and undoubtedly seriously damaged al-Qaeda in Iraq, but it's highly likely that they helped generate the rise of the Islamic State of Iraq and Syria (ISIS), al-Qaeda's successor in the region.

Regardless of any long-term strategic failings, though, JSOC was incredibly effective in removing bad guys from the battlefield. It was 'a force of unprecedented agility and lethality', according to Peabody Award–winning journalist Peter Bergen, and this was, in no small part, thanks to General Stanley McChrystal.

When he arrived in Afghanistan, McChrystal was a staunch proponent of COIN, but his version of the strategy involved just as much stick as carrot. McChrystal believed in building and mediating by day, and in killing and capturing by night.

In 2010, the *Rolling Stone* journalist Michael Hastings penned a now notorious profile of McChrystal (which became the basis of the Brad Pitt film *War Machine*), and he had this to say of the general:

Even in his new role as America's leading evangelist for counterinsurgency, McChrystal retains the deep-seated instincts of a terrorist hunter. To put pressure on the Taliban, he has upped the number of Special Forces units in Afghanistan from four to 19. 'You better be out there hitting four or five targets tonight,' McChrystal will tell a Navy Seal he sees in the hallway at headquarters. Then he'll add, 'I'm going to have to scold you in the morning for it, though.'

Because of this article, General McChrystal had a relatively short posting as ISAF commander, deposed for (among other alleged transgressions) badmouthing the US executive. His successor, General David Petraeus, continued the focus on COIN and employed a 'kill/capture' campaign. Under his tenure, the Joint Prioritized Effects List (JPEL) expanded significantly.

According to the notable Irish journalist Andrew Cockburn's book *Kill Chain: The Rise of the High-Tech Assassins*, there were 2058 Afghan men on the list marked for kill or capture in October 2009. Now it was not only Taliban fighters who were in the sights of ISAF, but also criminals, drug runners and other armed political opponents of the Karzai government. John Nagl, a former counter-insurgency advisor to General Petraeus, said that in Afghanistan the coalition special forces network became 'an almost industrial-scale counter-terrorism killing machine'.

The JPEL missions were undertaken by special forces soldiers across a range of units, task groups and nations including US Rangers, Delta Force, Navy Seals, British SAS, as well as the Australian SOTG. Although publicly there is an insistence that the priority for US and other coalition soldiers tasked with prosecuting the JPEL was to capture their objectives, it was usually safer to kill any combatants; as one Australian source quoted in a Fairfax report about the task force said, they 'don't take many prisoners'.

According to Bill Roggio, journalist and managing editor of *The Long War Journal*, 'in a six-month period in 2010 more than seven thousand special operation raids were conducted, resulting in thousands of Afghan dead, including over 600 Taliban leaders'. This does not include Taliban killed during conventional missions, nor retaliations when Taliban fighters attacked ISAF forces or civilians.

With the Australian SOTG in Tarin Kowt being one of the biggest special forces tribes in Afghanistan, there was no shortage of jobs for them. Cameron Baird's 2 Commando unit was gradually becoming a full-bore special forces unit equal to any in the country, and on this rotation they were transitioning from long, slow, dangerous vehicle missions to short, agile, adrenaline-fuelled helicopter tasks.

After the Kajaki job, the men of Bravo Company were called on to conduct a 15-day vehicle-borne clearance and interdiction operation. It was on this mission that Cam came to a point of personal crisis, but also of professional maturation.

—

Two of Cam Baird's defining traits as a soldier were that he would never badmouth another soldier behind his back, especially a superior, and that he was convinced the chain of command was essential to effective operating.

As this latest rotation progressed, Cam became increasingly concerned about the actions of his team commander, who was also his immediate superior. Cameron felt this soldier was badmouthing command, thus creating a negative environment for the men under him, and that he had started making decisions that were tactically unsound.

Cam knew that risk was part of the job for any soldier, but he believed that in any instance where there was risk, there must also be commensurate reward. Cam felt that his team commander had started to lose his appreciation of that ratio.

Richie Young, a senior team commander at the time, says he understood the conflict Cam was wrestling with. 'We were in a VDO [vehicle drop-off],' he says, 'and Cam was on piquet [guard], sitting in the cupola on the 50 [mm machine gun]. I was saying g'day to the boys, making sure everything's square, and I pulled up next to him. "You all good, man?" "Yeah, all good, all good." I thought that something was on his mind, though. I could tell he wanted to say something. I knew something may not be quite right.'

Later in the mission, Cam's team was to be split into two for an action, with Cam commanding three soldiers and his commander commanding three others. Once again, Richie could tell that Cam was worried.

'I said, "Mate, what's going on?" and he said, "No, it's okay, it's okay." It literally took me ten minutes to get it out of him,' he recalls. 'I said, "I'm worried that you're worried," because Cam would usually always speak his piece.'

Cam told Richie that he was concerned about the actions of his team commander. This was an exceptionally difficult thing for him to speak about. The man was his immediate superior, and Cam's instinct was to support him, but he couldn't do that when he thought he was putting his men in unnecessary peril.

'I gave him the out,' Richie continues. 'I said, "Do you want me to go and take care of it?" I knew full well that he was never going to say, "Yeah." He was man enough to take care of it himself.'

Before he did anything, Cam informed his team commander face-to-face of what he was planning to say. He then went up the chain of command and recommended to his officers that this man should relinquish his command – a very serious action at any time, let alone while on deployment to a combat zone.

A decision was made almost immediately to remove the soldier and install Cam as the team commander. As soon as the decision was made, Cam called a meeting with his team and told them exactly what had happened. He didn't detail the specific concerns he'd raised, but he did stress that he was the one who'd had an issue with the previous commander.

'It all made sense. In fact, I was immensely proud of the way he dealt with it,' says Young. 'He already had the respect of the boys, and now it was his turn to do things his own way.' Cam's leadership style, Young says, was very much by example – and usually that meant leading from the front. 'When it comes to planning, if there was a most dangerous area, he'd always put himself there. Especially if it was Cam's plan. He was never going to send his boys somewhere he wouldn't go himself.'

Santi Sambara, now a team commander himself, says he learned a lot about the Afghanistan War and warfighting while working under Cam – not only about setting an example, but also about when to defer and when to let his charges off the leash. Some soldiers, he says, considered that the war started and ended when they passed through the gates (or airspace) of the base in Tarin

Kowt, but not Cameron Baird. As soon as he left Australia for Afghanistan he was in warrior mode, with every movement and every decision, even in his downtime, dedicated to ensuring his ascendancy over the enemy.

When Cam became team commander, he made himself available to his team at any time, and was happy to talk about any aspect of the war. He even instituted a 'team night' in Tarin Kowt, which usually consisted of crowding around a laptop and watching schlock action films that, Santi says, could only be described as B-grade if you were feeling generous.

'The intel was pretty bad then,' Santi says, 'and a lot of the job was to basically go out to the "badlands" and see what we could see. Cam would often see us dishevelled because we'd been out all night, fighting all night for nothing and fatigued as hell, and he knew we'd need a pep talk. He'd sit down and explain why we were doing what we were doing, and what we were trying to do, and he made it all make sense.'

Part of the frustration for the men of Bravo, Cam included, was that they were so close to the kinds of missions that they wanted to be a part of: helicopter-borne assaults. This desire wasn't only because they wanted to strike swiftly and 'without warning' – the meaning of the commando regiment's motto, *foras admonitio* – but also because flying in on a target largely mitigated the IED threat.

The commandos truly hated IEDs. No one wanted to die in Afghanistan, but to die from an IED was particularly a shitty fate. Going face-to-face in a gunfight was fair play as far as most were concerned, but dropping explosives across the countryside and just waiting for someone to have their limbs or life sacrificed for no strategic reason was just scumbaggery. Cam, though, had a more nuanced view.

'We were in our room once bitching about the IEDs,' says Santi, 'and Cam said that if the roles were reversed, we would be doing the same shit. He said, "If someone invaded Australia and we were soldiers out in the winds we'd be doing the exact same shit. They're in a no-holds-barred fight. We are constrained in what we can do, but they're not. Women, children, animals, whatever – it's all fair play as far as they're concerned." For me and the younger guys, the war seemed to make a little bit more sense after that.'

Finally, the commandos got what they wanted. During Rotation Nine, Bravo Company started doing helicopter-borne operations, which would henceforth become the standard. And as soon as they started getting the air assets they were looking for, the results followed.

'As team commanders, we started being able to do a dedicated analysis of the terrain, being able to use deception with different aircraft, being able to insert and have some flexibility with our planning,' Richie Young says. 'We got rid of that large, telegraphed footprint and we started to see a lot more success.'

Cam and his team would have to wait for the next rotation, however, to conduct airborne assaults. Even so, Baird was relishing command, forging his team into the kind of warfighters he wanted them to be.

Sometimes (but rarely) when the fighting started, Cam would hold back, just a little, in order to push his guys forward. Santi Sambara was happy to do so, knowing it was what Cam wanted, but also because he knew he had the support of his experienced team commander, who was always within shouting distance. Santi particularly remembers one incident in this period, the effects of which made Cam the happiest he had ever seen him.

Both Cam's and Richie's teams were conducting a clearance in the Mirabad Valley when the Taliban opened up on them. The enemy's main offensive weapon was a PK machine gun, and the fire caught one of the commando snipers in the neck. This was likely supposed to be a classic 'shoot and scoot' attack, hitting the commandos with a heavy weapon and then melting away before there could be a response.

'When the gun opened up, our whole team's instinct was to run forward and run at the contact,' says Santi. 'Everyone else stopped – there was a team with us and they stopped – but our team split into our pairs and did our thing. We were doing two-man clearances and jumping over walls, shooting at dudes. Cam was running behind us, which he almost never [did], literally cheering us along the way.

'We ended up running over the top of this dude. He was oblivious to us being there because we moved up so quickly. Timmy [Aplin] ended up killing him, and Cam was running around the whole team, high-fiving us.'

'You guys are mad cunts. I didn't have to tell you anything and you all just split up and ran forward,' Cam said.

'I reckon that's as happy as I've ever seen him,' Santi recalls. 'He'd bred us to be fearless fighters.'

Richie Young agrees. 'My team came round the corner,' he remembers, 'and there was a dead machine-gunner and Cam was like, "Mate, look at this Cheshire cat." I reckon Cam was as happy as Timmy was.'

Richie's assessment of his mate is simple. 'He was just born to lead,' he says. 'Everyone was a better soldier for being in Cam's team. Blokes would literally die for him, and I reckon it's because they knew, if it came to it, he'd absolutely do the same.'

CHAPTER TWELVE

TO HELMAND AND BACK

'They were instant-gratification missions. You go there at night, fuck up a bunch of shit, blow up drugs, ruin some bad dude's week . . . you were basically Batman.'

TIM STANTON

TARIN KOWT, AFGHANISTAN
2011–12

Back in 1981, while Kaye and Doug were preparing to welcome their second child down in Burnie, in the American south Keith Bishop's life was changing too. After an exceptional run in the offensive line at Baylor University, Texas, the square-jawed, 191-centimetre, 120-kilogram giant was about to move to Colorado, where he would play in the Denver Broncos' offensive line.

Bishop spent ten years' worth of winter Sundays protecting Hall of Fame quarterback John Elway, with the pair reaching two Super Bowls. Along the way, Bishop played in two Pro Bowls.

When, in 1989, it came time for Bishop to retire from football, he looked for a career that offered similar action and significance. Eventually, he joined the Drug Enforcement Administration (DEA).

In 1980 the life of a young Afghan boy named Shah Afghani was changing too. The Soviet Army had invaded his country and, with the 11-year-old's father having worked at the US embassy and a purge of pro-American Afghans in full swing, he and members of his family were planning to flee to Pakistan.

Eventually the family ended up relocating to the United States, where Afghani lived a very American life. But he could never forget his homeland, and how narcotics and the money it had brought with it had enabled the endless fighting, which had been going on well before the Soviet invasion. When Afghani finished school, he too joined the DEA.

Keith Bishop and Shah Afghani combined at the agency's regional office in Kabul in 2010, Bishop as the assistant regional director and Afghani as a special agent. It was a professional partnership par excellence at a time when there were as many pitfalls as opportunities for the organisation.

For almost 20 years Afghanistan had been the largest producer of heroin in the world, often making nine times more heroin than the rest of the world combined. The only year that Afghanistan had not been the world's primary producer of heroin was in 2000, when the Taliban government forbade farmers to cultivate poppies in Afghan fields, under penalty of death. The year before, Afghanistan had produced over 3000 tons of processed heroin; in 2000 that figure fell to an estimated 185 tons. Then in 2001 the Taliban were deposed, and the very next year more than 3000 tons of processed heroin was produced again. Thus, the American assault proved to be a great boon for the drug kingpins of Afghanistan.

'Drug control wasn't a priority,' Jean-Luc Lemahieu, head of the United Nations' Office on Drugs and Crime in Afghanistan from 2009 to 2013, told *Rolling Stone* in December 2014. 'Limiting casualties was, and if that meant engaging in unholy alliances with actors of diverse plumage, such was the case.'

Since the US invasion, poppy cultivation has increased most years, thanks to both the Taliban and the US government showing a willingness to partner with the worst narco-barons in the country. The Americans pinned their nation-building hopes on Hamid Karzai, a man whose brother was almost certainly in bed with the biggest heroin traffickers in the world, while the Taliban started running their own huge heroin operations in southern Afghanistan, having lost much of the revenue that they needed to fund their endless war (although they still collected tax in large swathes of the country).

When Keith Bishop got to Kabul, it wasn't his job to worry about the corrupt and labyrinthine politics of Afghanistan; his mission was stopping heroin from getting to the United States. To that end, he decided he needed two things: intelligence and combat assets. The DEA had developed a giant intelligence network in Afghanistan, but there were arguably no parts more important than those managed by his colleague Shah Afghani.

Afghani was an American and a DEA agent through and through, having worked for years in the United States on domestic counter-narcotics operations. But he was also an Afghan who spoke Dari and Pashto, and he had family links to some of the most powerful families in the country.

For Bishop, teaming up with Afghani meant one side of his needs – intelligence – would be met. Combat assets were another matter, though. Burning a poppy field was relatively easy, and usually brought no more resistance than a single irate farmer could muster, but the DEA wanted to attack the processing centres, the last stop for Afghanistan's heroin before it was shipped out of the country. With tens of millions of dollars' worth of product being moved through these locations, the Taliban and the drug lords kept them well guarded.

The DEA had money and could put together a fleet of helicopters and drones, and had a relatively deep roster of experienced pilots, but they didn't have expert gunfighters. The agency did have some paramilitary operators in Afghanistan, but they weren't numerous or experienced enough for the task.

In 2009, when President Obama announced that there would be a surge in the number of American troops in Afghanistan, the DEA hoped that some would be available to help with its counter-narcotics operations. But each request was spurned. There were too many unholy alliances and, politically, it was far more important to keep coalition casualties down.

Bishop and the DEA weren't giving up, though, so they looked to international special forces units. They partnered with Norwegian and New Zealand special forces in operations around Kabul, but what the agency really needed was men who could go into the southern province of Helmand.

Helmand was the global epicentre of poppy culti-vation and heroin production. Despite being smaller than Tasmania, it produced approximately 40 per cent of global heroin supply. If ever there was an actual war on drugs, then Helmand would be the front line.

It was here that the relationship between 2 Commando and the DEA formed. Shah Afghani had travelled to Kandahar to participate in a meeting to discuss the nexus between the insurgency and drug production in the south. There he met Captain John Valentine, 2 Commando's plans officer, whose role included looking at how drug produc-tion was affecting security in Uruzgan.

Theirs was the first of many close friendships that were formed between the DEA and the commandos. The Australian SOTG had long understood that much of the insurgency was paid for by the drug trade, and they were doing counter-nexus operations of their own, but they lacked the necessary intel and air assets that would enable them to attack the trafficking networks.

Talk of the DEA and 2 Commando working together went up the ranks in both organisations. Eventually Keith Bishop had discussions with Greg Barton, who by then had replaced Valentine as the 2 Commando plans officer, and was soon to become the Commander of Bravo Company.

I met Barton – a thoughtful but matter-of-fact man with impeccable posture, prematurely grey hair and an athletic build – in his office at Russell, Canberra. He's a man who will, according to his superiors, likely one day be the overall commander of the 2nd Commando unit. He was the officer in command of Cameron Baird's last mission.

'[The DEA] is an organisation of 5500 people working in 65 countries, so they don't have much capacity to prosecute the intelligence that they generate,' Barton says. 'To work efficiently they have to develop networks and relationships, and those networks and relationships are incredibly important to them. [John Valentine] was in the right place at the right time. [The DEA] had exhausted their American special forces options and it was lucky for everyone that we had shared interests.'

Barton was personally excited about the prospect of a partnership. In a war with many shades of grey, attacking these drug networks looked like a decidedly black-and-white action. What was more, plenty of the heroin produced in Afghanistan ended up in Sydney and Melbourne and other Australian cities, and the cash it produced funded the insurgents. Destroying the heroin would not only be denying the Taliban bombs and bullets, it would also be squeezing the Australian drug market.

For the gunfighters of 2 Commando, men like Cameron Baird, the greatest attraction of these missions was that they would take them into Helmand and the thick of the fighting.

—

The approval process began. For the Australians to work with the DEA, it needed to be proven that each mission would be an effective use of resources and contribute to the nation's goals in Afghanistan. Drug eradication was not an overall goal, so that meant that it had to be proven that by working with the DEA in Helmand these soldiers would be contributing to the security of Uruzgan in a more significant way than if they were tasked with traditional counter-insurgency missions.

On 6 June 2011, while this was being finalised, Australian special forces Sapper Rowan Robinson was shot and killed in operations in Helmand. Keith Bishop flew down to Tarin Kowt in one of the DEA's fleet of Beechcraft King Air dual-prop planes so he could attend the ramp ceremony and pay his respects. While in Uruzgan, he, Barton and other commando leaders hammered out the first cooperative counter-nexus operations with the DEA.

'[Bishop is a] big, white, six-foot-three, ex–NFL player, very imposing dude, but he just took me under his wing,'

Barton says. 'The DEA people were having troubles getting their own country to support them, and they had these Australians saying yes. They were very appreciative.'

In one of the first inter-organisational briefings, Barton gave a DEA team commander an outline of how the Australians could support them. The American was expecting six to twelve guys, but instead he was offered all of Bravo Company, or almost 100 gunfighters. At first he thought Barton was joking.

'He thanked me for the combat support, and I said I thought that was the first time in history that an American had thanked an Australian for combat support,' laughs Barton.

The 2 Commando unit was seizing every opportunity for kinetic action. Exercises and courses were something, but there was never going to be any substitute for 'down-range' (or combat) operations, especially high-tempo downrange operations. In 2011 that meant helicopters, and that meant Helmand.

With the combat support in Helmand that its leaders had been yearning for, the DEA was spinning up as many large operations as they could. The missions were going to be classic special forces, with all the intelligence and air platforms that they entailed.

By the time Cam and the commandos of Bravo Company arrived in Afghanistan, they knew that these counter-nexus missions were to be a very large part of their workload. They were frothing with excitement.

'When we arrived it was the peak of the surge, and Uruzgan was basically locked down,' says Tim Stanton, who by this time was also one of Bravo's team commanders. 'The police had checkpoints all down the Mirabad Valley, and we couldn't even get into a gunfight in Uruzgan, so just as well we got to push out.'

Bravo's missions were split into two groups, designated *Markhanuel* and *Seratophin*. Seratophin missions were direct counter-insurgency missions, often cordon, sweep or capture/kill operations similar to the missions that Cam had undertaken during his previous rotation. Markhanuel missions were the anti-nexus missions conducted with the DEA.

Every team in the unit was trying to get as many of these Markhanuel missions as possible. Not only was Uruzgan relatively peaceful, the intelligence in the region had become spotty, and when the commandos came into an Afghan compound for a Seratophin mission, more often than not they would find nothing more than terrified farmers and their wives and children. Markhanuel

Cameron Baird consults a map during Bravo Company's final Afghan Rotation.

Cam with his beloved 1928 Ford Hiboy Roadster, powered by a 5.8 litre V8 351 Cleveland motor. A couple of high-performance classics.

After going through a tough year, Brendan and Cameron travelled to the resort town of Phuket, Thailand, in January 2013. The ocean was blue, the beer cold and the brothers spent their days visiting temples, bars and beaches.

Baird was described as a born leader. Here he poses with his assault team shortly after becoming a team commander.

'Learned extrovert' Cameron Baird instructs a group of Afghan commandos.

Baird with best mate Eddie Robertson, both wearing their deployment beards.

The gunfighters of Bravo Company.

Vehicle commander Cameron Baird does a navigation check in Helmand Province.

Cameron Baird
ready for battle.

The 'Iron Maiden' trio of Cam Baird, Timothy 'Aps' Aplin and Mervyn 'Merv' McDonald – three blokes who loved a laugh, heavy metal music and, above all, relentless, forward-foot fighting. By July 2013 all three would be dead.

An honour guard of commandos bring Cameron Baird's body back to Australia, his duty now done.

Cam Baird's M4 rifle sitting below an image of Baird and some of the men he fought with on his final day.

In 2014, Kaye and Doug travelled to Turkey and met Guven Pinar, whom Cam had billeted with. Guven gave Kaye the mug Cameron used during his stay.

'Team Cam's Cause' – (*clockwise from top left*) Chris Dyer, Daniel Carroll, Andrew Harrison, Rick Green. Honouring their fallen mate.

In November 2014, the Governor-General of Australia, Peter Cosgrove, Lady Cosgrove and Doug and Kaye Baird unveiled a life-size statue of Cameron at Currumbin Returned Services Club in Queensland.

missions, however, almost always meant action, gunfights and phenomenal air support.

The DEA didn't have much access to US military air assets, so they had rented or bought their own fleet of aircraft, including a grab bag of tactical transport helicopters that they used for assaults on drug locations. The bulk of these aircraft were Russian Mi-17 helicopters, which had been the workhorse of the Soviet invasion of Afghanistan.

Anything the Mi-17 lacked in manoeuvrability, compared with the American Black Hawks, was more than made up for by the skill and daring of the contracted DEA pilots who operated the aircraft. Quite a bit older than the US military pilots who usually ferried the commandos to and from their missions, most of the DEA contractors were retired pilots with experience in one or both Iraq conflicts; some had even flown in Vietnam. They were men with bulging biceps, grey beards and a natural maverick spirit that had been honed further by age – the commandos dubbed them 'The Expendables'.

These pilots were uniformly described by the commandos I interviewed as the best they'd ever worked with. The Mi-17 has a reputation for being able to take an exceptional amount of damage before falling out of the sky, and that fact, combined with the experience of the pilots and a near-complete dearth of flying restrictions, meant that insertions, exfiltrations and medical evacuations during the Markhanuel missions were always as easy as they could be.

'The difference between getting in their birds and any other helos was amazing,' says Tim. '"You tell us where you want to go, and we'll put you there. Whatever you want, you can have it." They were fucking awesome.'

Dan Laguna was one of the contracted pilots. 'When I asked [a team commander] how close he wanted me to get him to the target, he said as close as I could,' he recalls. 'So [I] put him at the front door – he had the element of surprise on the bad guys. He told me no one has ever put him that close; he was a happy man.'

Laguna, a legendary former Green Beret operator in the 1970s, became a pilot for the US Special Operations Aviation Regiment after his brother Art, himself a pilot, bet him he couldn't graduate flight school. Laguna flew special-operations missions in Iraq during Desert Shield, in Bosnia, in Somalia (on rescue missions after his friend Michael Durant was shot down and then taken hostage in the incident that inspired the film *Black Hawk Down*), and in the recent Iraq War (where he watched Art's chopper get gunned down and all on board die while flying next to him).

Laguna admired the commandos as much as they did him. '[The men of 2 Commando] are very good at their job, some of the best I have worked with in my 40 years doing SPECOPS missions,' he says.

The Markhanuel missions were conducted alongside small Foreign-deployed Advisory and Support Team (FAST) units, who were DEA special agents trained to work in combat zones, and Afghans from the DEA's partner force, the Nation Interdiction Unit (NIU), a force that was being trained to take over the work of the Americans when they left the country.

It was usually mandated that the commandos took members of their partner force, the Provincial Response Company (PRC), on operations, but in the confusing tapestry of ancient Afghan hatreds, the men of the Kabul-based NIU and the men of the Uruzgan-based PRC were at odds, so the Australians were often relieved of that responsibility.

The missions evolved as follows: intelligence was gathered, often from Shah Afghani's network of spies and informants, but sometimes directly from competing drug networks. The DEA used the intelligence to best effect, which didn't always mean instantly prosecuting it. The DEA held off from raids until they knew they would be striking when the greatest amount of processed drugs, precursors and money was on site. They also sometimes left a specific network unmolested, in the hope that rival syndicates might assume it was working with the DEA and attack it.

When the DEA operators were ready to execute a mission they put together a 'target package'. Using satellite and drone imagery, as well as any intelligence, the package would specify what equipment and materials the DEA expected to find, what kind of resistance might be expected and how the site related to the insurgency. These packages would be shared with Bravo, and a mission plan formulated.

On the ground, the job of the Australians was essentially to take on all the gunfighting and most of the demolition work. After landing, the Aussie chalks would be tasked with setting up cordons and clearing the compounds within, killing anyone who offered resistance. When the area was relatively safe, the FAST team would gather evidence, question and detain suspects and direct the Australians to the materials that needed to be destroyed.

Initially the missions were similar to airborne counter-insurgency missions – in fact, some of the labs were guarded by Taliban fighters – but as they did more missions the Australians gained a greater understanding of the drug production process. Towards the end of the rotation, they knew which precursor chemicals and what type of equipment was essential and rare, and therefore had to be destroyed.

'Sometimes they'd resist, sometimes not, but we were inside the curve of them adapting to us, and that rotation we made hay,' Tim Stanton recalls. 'I remember one of the best nights: we rolled through five or six compounds in a valley and, as we flew away, from the back of the chopper you could see a burning path where we'd destroyed labs and drugs. They were instant-gratification missions. You go there at night, fuck up a bunch of shit, blow up drugs, ruin some bad dude's week . . . you were basically Batman.'

Bravo Company did more missions that summer than on any of their other rotations, and while the soldiers were regularly in gunfights, resulting in scores of Taliban killed, they had very few casualties. All in all, it was a great rotation for the gunfighters and for command. Not only did the company regularly get into situations that would cost millions to emulate in training, they also proved themselves exemplary in missions that were being talked about in the highest echelons of American government. Hundreds of millions of dollars' worth of drugs were destroyed, and the means of future production went up in smoke with them.

'Part of our overall mission in Afghanistan was to support the Americans,' says Greg Barton, 'and these

[DEA-cooperative] operations were huge. They were mentioned in Congress, so this was a big tick.'

Keith Bishop remembers the Australian commandos as one of the most professional and adaptable special forces outfits that the DEA worked with in his time. 'With them it was always just a constant positive, can-do attitude,' he says. 'Whatever we wanted to do, their answer was always, "Let's do it – we'll figure out a way." Working with them was one of the most outstanding things I did in my career.'

—

The Markhanuel operations were Cameron Baird's favourite missions on his favourite rotation. Not only did he improve his practical gunfighting skills, he also honed his demolition skills. They were all airborne missions, too, which often meant dinner in Tarin Kowt, mission, breakfast in Tarin Kowt. This was quite a contrast to the previous rotation, with its long, multi-day drives made tense by the IED threat.

Cam spent a lot of his spare time reading. The men remember him lost in Homer's epic poem *The Iliad*, the pop-economics book *Freakonomics* and a self-help book entitled *How to Talk to Anyone: 92 Little Tricks for Big Success in Relationships*.

Cameron perhaps chose that last book because he had started to mentor Afghan troops – from both the PRC and the NIU. The book may also have appealed because Cam had probably, as one of his officers suggests, learned to be an extrovert. A naturally inquisitive man, he would have appreciated the opportunity to interact socially with the Afghans while mentoring them.

Another book Cam enjoyed on that rotation was *Cave in the Snow*, the biography of a Buddhist yogini. Cam had been developing an interest in Eastern philosophy since high school. When pursuing exercises that might help improve his football, he'd heard about a minor trend in professional football circles for yoga. He became a practitioner himself. Among his friends and contemporaries there were precisely zero others with this interest, but Cam routinely contorted his giant body through downward dog, sarvangasana and ustrasana.

Although on the surface Cam seemed to have a natural equanimity, it seems that it, like his extroversion, was learned. He told those closest to him that anger and aggression were factors of his personality that he was always trying to control. There are almost no instances of Cameron being outwardly out of control or rage-filled – especially not when in combat – but he was always looking for ways to control his anger.

Perhaps this was why he loved books about people controlling their circumstances and mood through enlightened thought. Perhaps this was why he particularly resonated with *Cave in the Snow*. It told the story of a young British woman, originally named Diane Perry, who entered an Indian monastery, took the name Tenzin Palmo and lived alone, for more than a decade, in a freezing cave in the Himalayas, 4000 metres above sea level.

'He idolised that chick,' Jack Ducat says. 'One morning we were waiting to go up in a chopper and it's pelting down snow, and Cam is just wearing a combat shirt, shaking, and I had a huge puff jacket. I asked, "Why are you not wearing a jacket?" and he said, "Don't need one, mate." He was shivering like a leaf. "[Tenzin] doesn't need a jacket. I don't either." I said, "Mate, she's not waiting to go in a helicopter in Afghanistan in winter."'

The pragmatic Jack was the perfect foil for Cam, with his flights of philosophical fancy. In the team commanders' room on the base, Cam, Jack, Tim Stanton and the other leaders would talk about how they should develop their tactics in an ever-evolving battlespace, but also generally about life and death.

Once Cam was talking to the others about how he'd realised people needed very little to live a happy life. He talked about the simple life, the ascetic life, which Tenzin

Palmo had lived and which, to a lesser extent, the soldiers lived when on deployment. Luxuries quite often ended up becoming complications, Cam said, and a negative force in one's life.

When he finished speaking there was a moment of quiet reflection and appreciation, until Jack Ducat broke the silence. 'You do love your hot rod, though.'

'Oh, yeah, I fucking love my hot rod.'

He did, too. There were few civilian enterprises that Cam enjoyed more than getting into his immaculately clean and detailed orange 1928 Ford Hiboy Roadster, donning his flat cap – which made him seem far older than he actually was – and driving into the countryside around Sydney.

This was not only the most successful rotation for Bravo, but also the longest. Snow usually starts to fall in Afghanistan in late October or early November, making many of the roads into Pakistan impassable, and long journeys within the country difficult. At that point, the fighting usually starts to wind down. Assassinations and suicide bombings continue in urban areas, but in the countryside Taliban activity slows, not resuming until the annual 'spring offensive', sometime in April.

That winter, however, was a very mild one, and with the snow coming exceptionally late, the Taliban and the commandos extended their fighting season. Normally at the start of winter 2 Commando would be replaced by 1 Commando, a reserve unit of part-time soldiers who operated at a slower tempo. Instead, Bravo drew down to a platoon-size – around 40 soldiers – and remained in country.

Sitting with the other remaining team commanders, Cam watched the rest of the company pack into a C-130. As it took off and wheeled to the south, the first hop on the way back to Australia, Cam shook his head and said, with compassion in his voice, 'Imagine being one of those dickheads having to go home.'

—

During the winter months, the remaining Aussie commandos maintained an unprecedented pace, ticking off a long list of missions that were desirable, if not essential. When Cam and the last Bravo men left Tarin Kowt, the company had sustained no fatalities.

It had been a successful and satisfying rotation, but after nearly eight months of fighting, most of the guys were keen to head home to their partners and children. Jack said to Cam that even he must be looking forward to the peace and quiet of Sydney.

'I'm looking forward to seeing my dogs,' came the reply. Cam and Robin had two small, fluffy dogs – pets quite at odds with the image of Cameron Baird the big, burly soldier, but perfectly in line with the reality of Cameron Baird the contrarian. 'They look forward to seeing you no matter what,' he said.

Cam was a stoic, and was ever reluctant to talk to anyone about personal matters; this comment was a rare instance in which he hinted at difficulties in his personal life. When he returned to Australia in February 2012, he must have known that re-entering the routine of married life would be difficult. He had no idea, however, just how tumultuous that year would turn out to be.

CHAPTER THIRTEEN

2.0

'God, I loved that boy.'

KRISTINA 'CRICKET' TYREE

In the same week that Cam deployed for Afghanistan in mid-2011, Brendan's wife was told she was seriously ill. Only a few weeks after that, doctors told Brendan there was no way of saving his wife.

There were of course many family concerns. It was a fraught time and one of the many questions was whether to tell Cam that his sister-in-law was going to pass away before he returned to Australia. Doug and Kaye thought that perhaps it would be better not to tell him – that they should break it to him when he got back.

But Brendan insisted Cam be told immediately, so that he could say his goodbyes. Throughout their lives, Brendan argued, his and Cam's brotherhood had been based on trust. Obscuring the truth would make everything worse for both men. Brendan's wife was dying – there was no getting away from that fact.

Brendan and Cam had spoken semi-regularly while Cam was on deployment. In December, Brendan told Cam that his wife was dying, and very quickly. If Cam wanted to speak to his sister-in-law one last time, he would have to do it soon.

Unprepared for this news, Cam sat in a small room in Camp Russell and, with war all around him, was struck dumb. When the words came, Cam said he would call Brendan back. Five minutes later, Brendan's phone rang. Cam and his sister-in-law had their last conversation, the contents of which will never be known.

'I remember telling him he needed to keep focus. "I can deal with this – you just have to concentrate over there,"' Brendan says. 'He was pretty upset he couldn't be there for me.'

On 12 December 2011, shortly after that final phone call with Cam, Brendan's wife died. It was doubtless a confronting moment for Cameron. He had almost finished a rotation that was unarguably the most successful and satisfying he'd had. Bravo was operating at an incredibly high tempo and with devastating efficacy, and was yet to sustain any combat casualties. Now death had hit him anyway, from the home front. Relatively slow but inexorable, it was a death that was in stark contrast to those the commandos had become accustomed to.

Cam was not able to attend the funeral. The day after he returned from Afghanistan, he flew straight to Melbourne, where Brendan was packing up his house. He and his sons were relocating to be closer to Kaye and Doug, who were able to give ongoing unconditional support throughout this difficult time for the Baird family.

Cam and Brendan were together in north-west Melbourne again, but the suburb felt different. While the footy fields, takeaway shops and red-brick houses were the same, the Baird boys were not. The years since Cam had left Gladstone Park had hardened both men. Brendan was a widower, Cam a veteran. Each bore a great deal of weight on his shoulders.

Even through his grief, Brendan says, he could tell something was unsettled in his brother's life. Cam was hurting because of the pain Brendan and his children were going through, but it wasn't only that. Brendan knew it could only be either Cam's work or his marriage.

Brendan asked about work. Work was great, Cam told him. Best rotation yet – everyone came back and they kicked the Taliban right in the dick. After hearing that, Brendan knew it had to be Cam's marriage to Robin that was troubling him. He tried to broach the subject but Cam brushed it off. 'I'm not here to talk about me. I'm here for you, mate,' he told Brendan.

Three days after Cam left Melbourne, Brendan decided to fly to Sydney to talk some more to his brother. 'I could tell there was something he really had to get off his chest,' he says. 'I went with him to a pub in Mount Annan and he told me it was over with Robin. When he came back from Afghanistan, something had happened suddenly, and she was moving out.'

Robin told Doug and Kaye later that she wanted the marriage to persevere and that the split had been Cam's choice. The catalyst and particulars of any marriage break-up are difficult to distinguish, and without moving into the realm of speculation, we can say that in Cameron and Robin's marriage there was a decisive, revelatory moment that prompted the split.

The separation was heartbreaking in its ease. For pragmatic reasons, their marriage had been technically annulled years earlier, so their partnership required nothing more than Cam leaving the house for half a day so Robin could move her things out.

'He called and said, "I've left her,"' Kaye recalls. '"She's coming over to our house to take whatever she wants. I've left her a letter. I still care about her, but it's over and you might like to ring her, to say goodbye." We were in shock.'

Cam suggested that Robin should stay in the house while they put it on the market, but she refused. Robin may have wanted to keep the union intact, but she knew that when Cam made a decision he was not going to change his mind.

Cam had been with Robin for most of his adult life and, now, at age 31, he was suddenly alone. It was a seismic lifestyle change. Previously there had been weeks, and sometimes months, it seemed, when Cam and Robin would disappear into their home lives, enjoying a simple, domestic routine, punctured infrequently by counter meals at the pub, or perhaps a 'special occasion' night at the nearby Rydges Hotel. Now all that was gone.

The men of Bravo knew what had happened, and a few asked the burly team commander if he wanted to vent about his relationship. Cam always politely declined, going about his business on the base with his usual focus. Cam also declined to talk to Brendan about it.

He went up to the Gold Coast and saw Doug and Kaye, but he was reticent to talk to them, too, about the split.

'We wanted to know what had happened,' Doug says. 'He said, "Right, you have one opportunity and one opportunity only to talk about this. That moment is right now.

When we leave this table, we're never talking about this again." We were dumbfounded. It was very soldierly, and we didn't ask much.'

'It was only later,' Kaye admits, 'when we thought, *We should have asked this, we should have asked that.*'

About two weeks later, a new life started for Cameron Baird. His mates said he was reborn as 'Cam 2.0'.

'He just decided he was moving on in life,' Brendan says, 'and he didn't want to be in the dumps. He said his work was 100 per cent his priority, but he did want to meet someone and have a bit of fun. He said he just didn't want any, like, difficult stuff.'

No doubt Cam had moments of sadness and regret about his marriage ending, but he never articulated how he felt to those closest to him. In his work life and his private life, Cam rarely wavered from the 'next job' mentality that helped make him such an efficient soldier. And now he decided that his next job was to catch up on the single life that he'd missed out on while living a prematurely middle-aged suburban experience.

Cam started the process of remaking himself socially. He started to hit the gym with an extreme tempo, shaved carbs from his diet and added more protein. He planned to cover some of his tattoos (including one of Robin's name) with a contemporary, Japanese-style sleeve. He looked at real estate much closer to Sydney's centre. His place with Robin had been half an hour west of the Holsworthy Barracks, and it was another 45 minutes from there to Sydney's CBD. He wanted to be closer to the single blokes in the unit, and the haunts where they met young, urban women.

He even tried to revitalise his beer palate too, once going with a friend to the Belgian Beer Cafe in Sydney's CBD and asking for a 'fancy European beer'. When it came, it disgusted him so he sent it away and asked for a Victoria Bitter instead.

In March 2012 Cam joined eHarmony. In April he started chatting to an American 31-year-old systems engineer named Kristina Tyree. Cricket, as she was known, had lived and worked in Singapore, then moved to Sydney after meeting an Australian man in her industry. She decided the relationship wasn't for her, but the city and the new job was, so she stuck around.

Cricket was initially attracted to the straightforward charm of Cam's eHarmony profile, deciding to meet with him when she read his answer to the stock question 'What can't you live without?' His reply: 'Air. Food. Water.'

Cam was training out of Singleton at the time, in the Hunter Valley, and struggled to find a day when he could drive the two and a half hours down to the city after work and go on a date with Kristina. Eventually, they decided to meet at El Loco, a hip Mexican-themed restaurant and bar in Surry Hills.

A couple of days before the date, Cricket messaged Cam, suggesting they might need to relocate. It turned out they'd chosen to meet at the Mexican bar on Cinco de Mayo, a rambunctious, boozy holiday commemorating the Mexican Army's defeat of a French garrison at the Battle of Puebla. Cam said he had never heard of the battle or the holiday, but it all sounded right up his alley.

The pair found a relatively quiet spot at El Loco and started chatting. Cricket told Cam a bit about Singapore, and Cam answered a few questions about his work. Initially he was quite reserved, Cricket says, but she thought things were going quite well – until she noticed that he was regularly sneaking looks at his phone, which he was cradling in his lap.

'I'm pretty straightforward,' she remembers, 'so I said, "Dude, is this date not going great? Did you want to bail?"'

Cam was very apologetic, explaining that he was just checking the footy scores. The Crows were playing the Swans, and the sides had only one loss between them so far that season. She suggested that they go somewhere they could watch it together. So they repaired to a pub nearby and watched the game, with Cam explaining Aussie Rules to the slightly bewildered American.

'He was very patient and a really good explainer,' she says. 'The thing that struck me on that first date was that he was such a damn gentleman. He was a bit nervous and he was wearing his glasses and he just seemed so cute and innocent. It was when he stood up I'd be like, "Yeah, this dude is huge," but he was just a sweetheart.'

Before half time, Cam switched from beer to water. Cricket, who by then had decided she was making a night of it, asked why, and Cam told her he had to drive back to Mt Annan.

'I was pretty confident that he wasn't a psycho,' she says, 'so I told him that he could sleep on my couch.'

After the Crows won a narrow victory, they moved from the pub to the Gaslight Inn, a late-night joint across the road from Cricket's apartment. They drank thirstily and chatted easily until 4 a.m. Among many other things, they talked about their exes, although Cam was at pains not to badmouth Robin.

Cam wasn't one for telling his mates what was happening in his love life, but sometime between his first date with Cricket and his second, he had decided that he wanted to be in a relationship with her. For their second date, Cam took over a DVD of *Tour of Duty: Australia's*

Secret War, a documentary about the SOTG's operations in Afghanistan. Cam had been one of the interview subjects.

'He wasn't trying to big-note himself,' Cricket says. 'He just wanted to explain the kind of work he did, and most of all he wanted to explain that he was going to be away a lot, and that he wasn't always going to be in contact.'

Soon Cam was driving in to Sydney whenever he was free. Most weekends he would get in his car as soon as he finished work and drive from Singleton or Holsworthy to Darlinghurst for a couple of days of eating at 'hatted' restaurants such as Longrain or drinking at hole-in-the-wall bars specialising in revival cocktails like the Negroni or whiskey sour; Cam still preferred a VB. When the house he had shared with Robin was sold, Cam moved to Mascot, a much shorter drive to Kristina's place.

The civilian side of Cameron Baird's life had changed drastically, and soon, he knew, the military side would be transforming too. He was due to rotate back into Afghanistan in February 2013, for what would likely be his last trip as a door-kicking gunfighter.

Cam was soon to become a sergeant, a senior non-commissioned role that wouldn't take him as close to the fighting as he liked to be. According to his commander, Cam would likely have taken on the '1-1 role' – more or less the team commander of the team commanders – before migrating into a role at the Special Forces Training Centre in Holsworthy. Once he moved into that position he would no longer be fighting, but as an exemplary leader with a long and varied combat history, it was the best work he could do for the unit.

At 2 Commando in 2012, there was more opportunity to stave off rank than in other units at the time. A lot of the soldiers in the unit had become beret-qualified around the same time as Cam, and many had progressed in rank simultaneously with him. To avoid a glut of uniformed rank progressions, the leaders had deliberately staggered promotions across the unit. When Cam was informed that he would soon be expected to undertake the sergeants' course, his first thought was to put it off and stay at the heart of the fighting for a little longer.

Cam walked into Greg Barton's office and asked if he could stay unpromoted – and even if he could relinquish rank. He was almost laughed out of the room. His company commander asked him to explain the request. Cam replied that he thought that he lacked some specific capabilities, especially some close-quarters combat skills. His hope was that he could drop down in rank, complete some courses he hadn't yet done, and then, later, move towards a promotion to sergeant.

'As he talked, I was hard-pressed to keep a straight face because he was one of the most capable gunfighters I'd ever met,' says Barton.

Many of those in the unit have speculated that Cam tried to relinquish rank so he could stay a gunfighter. Some think it's because gunfighting had become his passion; others think it was where he thought his best skills lay, and therefore it was where he believed he could best serve the unit. A few think that Cam genuinely believed his skillset was lacking – not compared to the standards set by the regiment, but the standards he set for himself.

Cam had long felt that he'd missed some competencies when he was out of the unit after Iraq, while Bravo was working in 'black role' as members of TAG (East). Many of the courses the unit undertook during that period were in close-quarters battle situations. But Cam had been in a great deal of close-quarters combat – including the action in Chenartu, where he'd acted decisively and expertly – and he'd picked up most of the courses he'd missed. Still, he occasionally told people he felt he was lacking.

In 2010 Cam had fulfilled a rotation as a member of TAG (East), but it wasn't as the door-kicker he would have been if his Army career had progressed without interruption. Instead, he'd taken on the crucial role of Emergency Action commander, or EA.

TAG (East) has never been called into action (although its members were in communication with the New South Wales Police Force when lone gunman Man Haron Monis took hostages at the Lindt Café in Sydney's CBD in December 2014), but if they were, it would be the responsibility of the EA to devise a plan that the company commander would then execute, while a more comprehensive plan of action was formulated.

'The EA comes up with 60 per cent of a solution on time, which is far preferable to 100 per cent of a solution too late,' Barton says. 'They're selected for that job because they have something special. The learning curve is exponential, and it's a huge, high-stress responsibility.'

The EA has to be ready for a plan to be executed in any conceivable environment – aeroplane, airport, stadium, ship, office building, oil rig, nuclear reactor – against any number of enemy armed in any number of ways. It's a monumental job, requiring the synthesis of a huge amount of information about environments, tactics and weapon systems. What the EA is not responsible for, however, is tactical execution – close-quarters gunfighting.

When Cam walked into Barton's office, the company sergeant major, Bravo's most senior NCO, was also present. Neither he nor Barton was willing to entertain the thought of one of their most capable junior leaders refusing rank, so he laid out a counter-argument.

'Cam, you're a team commander – a big, imposing bloke with a bunch of soldiers below you who would follow you anywhere,' the CSM said. 'If you drop down, one of those guys has to try to be your team commander. What position does it put that dude in?'

After more discussion, Cam left the office apparently satisfied, and Barton was confident the issue had been quashed. It appears, however, that Cam then went over Barton's head, to the overall commander of 2 Commando, Lieutenant Colonel Tom Porter.

Although Porter commanded some 800 men and women – more than half of them gunfighters – he knew Cameron Baird quite well. Porter had been with the unit during its inception, before moving to Perth to work with the SASR. When he came back to 2 Commando in 2012, he knew about Cam and the action that had won him the Medal for Gallantry. Porter watched him work.

'[When coming into 2 Commando as the commanding officer] I had a "town hall" so the guys could shotgun me with any questions about how things were and how they would be,' Porter says. 'Straightaway he was that guy, peppering me. The questions were excellent, pertinent, so I used to say at the end of meetings, "Cam Baird – last word?" I had regular contact with him, and I'd use him to measure the temperature of the unit, which was especially useful in the last rots.'

That Cam went to Lieutenant Colonel Porter about his request to refuse rank was unusual behaviour for a soldier who believed so rigidly in the chain of command, but Cam was equally steadfast about doing what he saw to be the right thing. The fact that he did this adds credence to the view that he genuinely felt there were holes in his skillset. It's unlikely Cam would have ignored the chain of command purely to satisfy a personal wish.

Porter did much the same thing as Greg Barton and laughed Baird out of his office. He told me that he had some junior leaders in his unit who were as capable as Cam, but none was more capable. He thought the idea that Cam needed to go backwards before he could go forwards was absurd, and he told his charge exactly that. That was the end of it.

—

Cameron Baird was no longer married, and was now in a relationship with a woman who saw things very differently from his former partner. He was living close to the city for the first time, and he had a fair amount of disposable income. He had just one more tour left as the first bloke in the stink, but the other possibilities for his life were abundant.

'He was wondering what he was going to do next, and even talked about the possibility of getting a posting at Fort Bragg,' says Cricket.

Fort Bragg is a huge US military installation in North Carolina, housing (among others) the US Army Special Operations Command, or SOCOM. Cam was likely to have been talking about a secondment with 1st Group Green Berets, based in Washington State.

Cam had never been overseas except with the Army: one armed deployment to East Timor, one armed deployment to Iraq, three armed deployments to Afghanistan, and a very brief excursion to Turkey. It wasn't exactly what most Australians call travelling.

Cricket, on the other hand, was a very seasoned traveller, which stood in stark contrast to both Cam and Robin. She says Cam had question after question about the places she'd visited and wanted to visit, until eventually she asked him if he wanted to join her on a trip she was planning to her home city, Chicago.

A video montage of the trip (entitled 'America Fuck Yeah 2012') shows Cam and Cricket enjoying food, booze and each other from Chicago to Belize, with stops in Key

West, New Orleans and New York. In every shot, Cam is beaming from ear to ear.

'After that trip, the travel bug bit Cam, and it was a big bite,' Cricket says.

Cam returned from the United States in December 2012. He was due to be deployed in February 2013, but managed to arrange his schedule so he could have a few days off in January for a holiday in Thailand with Cricket, and also with Brendan. Cam felt it was time for his brother to move on from his grief, and think about his future.

The brothers had always been very different men, but their adult experiences had made them even more different in their temperaments. After his wife's death, sadness had seeped into every cell of Brendan's body – a sadness that weighed him down. Cam couldn't quite understand the depth of Brendan's grief. 'Brendan just needs to get over it and move on,' he told Cricket. Perhaps this was just Cam's natural disposition, reinforced by his years spent developing a commando's mentality. Like many of his comrades, Cam had a pragmatic attitude to death. It was an everyday aspect of their work and he didn't baulk when anyone talked about it. The dead died, and the living went on. That was just how it was.

In contrast to Brendan, it seemed that loss spurred Cam into action. This was exemplified in the way he memorialised the soldiers who had died in the Afghan conflict.

When Cameron's effects were delivered to his parents after his death, Doug and Kaye discovered a folder Cam had with him in Afghanistan. Inside were images of the Australian soldiers who had been killed there, alongside quotes and maxims about leadership and inspiration. It was one of the few personal items he had with him on that final rotation.

The Thailand trip was a smashing success. Brendan, Cam and Cricket travelled to the resort town of Phuket and spent their holiday visiting temples, bars and beaches. The ocean was blue and the beer was cold. Cam and Cricket had a carefree time, while Brendan at least had his mind elsewhere for a few days.

When Cam arrived back in Sydney, he started preparing for two journeys. One was to be a long European trip with Kristina: they planned to visit the United Kingdom, Italy, Spain and France. Cam had aspirations to learn at least the basics of all three foreign languages. One of the boys in Bravo Company describes being in the barracks toilet block and being disturbed by a booming 'Buenos días, señor' coming from the stall next door, followed by an equally emphatic 'Bonne journée, monsieur', then 'Buongiorno, signore'. The other journey was to be the familiar 'brown route' to Tarin Kowt, for Bravo Company's final rotation as part of ISAF.

While Cam was on deployment, Cricket would plan the details of their European trip, which they would enjoy before Cam took his sergeant's course. There were flights and accommodation to book, and she also wanted to research the historical and cultural sites the pair were keen to visit.

Another of Cricket's tasks while Cam was on deployment was to move out of her place and into his. Her rental lease was about to end, and rather than sign a new one, Cam suggested she should move in with him. 'No point in paying two rents,' he'd said. The offhand comment belied the significance of what their relationship had become.

Before the move, Cricket would be celebrating her 32nd birthday. A few days before his last deployment, Cam bought a pair of diamond earrings and hid them on top of a tall beam which cut across the lounge room in the diminutive American's apartment. 'He knew I wouldn't find them,' she says. 'I wasn't much of a one for dusting.'

Cam sent Cricket a note from Afghanistan, telling her where she would discover her present. When explaining the gesture to me, Cricket pauses in thought, then says: 'God, I loved that boy.'

CHAPTER FOURTEEN

A WINNABLE WAR

'My fellow Americans . . . even as there will be dark days ahead in Afghanistan, the light of a secure peace can be seen in the distance. These long wars will come to a responsible end.'
PRESIDENT BARACK OBAMA

TARIN KOWT, AFGHANISTAN
2013

The Afghanistan war wasn't ending, but it was ending for Australia. ISAF was being disbanded, and soon Afghans would be in charge of the fight against the Taliban. In Uruzgan that fight would largely be the responsibility of one man: Matiullah Khan, known to many as 'Australia's Warlord'.

Khan was a man with almost unparalleled power in southern Afghanistan. Once a taxi driver, the thirty-something Khan (his exact age wasn't known, apparently even to himself) was a self-made millionaire. He had been made very rich by Western standards – and immeasurably so by local ones – through taking payments from foreign governments to facilitate a modicum of safety and security in Uruzgan.

Khan's immense wealth was, in no small part, thanks to the Australian taxpayers, but whenever Australian politicians came to his compound – which had a rose garden, a swimming pool and a private mosque – he was short on thanks and long on reminders that they were guests in his country.

Aussie politicians were wary of Khan, unwilling to shake a hand stained by a bloody past. Khan, it had long been known, had killed political opponents, and there were persistent rumours that he used rape as a disciplinary measure, often administering the punishment personally. The man who laboured when signing official documents was not an archetypal Australian ally.

The authoritarian Khan may have killed and raped, but he was the best strategic partner available to Australia. He was what passed for Afghanistan's future hope, once the foreigners had left. Khan was the embodiment of the compromises Australia had been forced to accept in order to operate in Afghanistan.

Khan started to make a name for himself as the head of a ragtag highway patrol in 2001, obtaining the role after two fortunate events: the US invasion and the installation of Hamid Karzai, a tribal ally, as the nation's president. Khan and his men exerted surprising control over the lawless dirt roads of Uruzgan, and were merciless in their treatment of bandits and thieves.

Working as part security contractor, part standover man, Khan would charge exorbitant amounts to those who wanted to use 'his' roads, often smugglers and drug runners who'd pay up to get where they needed to go. When Khan's main clients became Western governments, he aggressively claimed that he no longer worked with those in the narcotics trade, but few believed him. It was also known that when Khan wasn't paid, the danger on the roads came not only from bandits but from Khan's own men.

Warrant Officer Class One Geoff Goddard OAM, currently the senior NCO of the Special Operations Command, remembers his first meeting with Khan while deployed on SOTG Rotation One. 'You'd go and have tea or a feed – a really nice feed – at his joint, and he'd have his hand resting on your leg and you'd feel like, *Hmm,*

I feel uncomfortable. He was this ex–taxi driver, [a] gangster who'd killed more people than Pol Pot. He was your friend now, but you just knew he was playing every angle in classic Afghan style.'

When Goddard went back for Rot Three, the American SEALs had decided it was perhaps time to kill Khan.

'They were saying, "I think we're going to take this guy down,"' Goddard recalls. 'They looked at the linkages and it was time for this guy to go. [That mission] got to the final stages before it got binned. All the other government agencies wanted to work with him, and they were thinking they were going to foster the next president of Afghanistan.'

The Australian Defence Force have stressed to me that they were not aware of any kill mission.

As Khan slowly built his wealth, he turned that capital into more men, arms and influence, until his force was the most powerful in Uruzgan Province. With Hamid Karzai's blessing, in 2011 Khan officially became the Uruzgan police chief, but in reality he was much more than that. By 2013 Khan had become a viceroy of sorts, helping to bring some security to the province, regularly convening shura and meting out justice as he saw it – as well as enriching himself to the tune of tens and perhaps hundreds of millions of dollars.

While Western politicians were wary of Khan, the military, especially those in charge of special forces units, often had a grudging respect for him. He was young for a warlord, and he was strong and fit and relatively effective. He also truly hated the Taliban, although he wouldn't have baulked at the opportunity to work with them if it suited his interests.

This was Khan's country; this was Khan's war. It was often difficult for the Australian soldiers to keep that fact in focus, as they'd killed and fought and watched friends die on Afghan soil. It felt like their war, but they were, in essence, participants in a civil conflict. This was becoming increasingly clear when Bravo arrived in Afghanistan for its final rotation.

'We had to push the Afghans up front,' says Lieutenant Colonel Tom Porter. 'A lot of us had to grow up. We had to realise [that] what was needed then wasn't what was needed now.'

And what was needed was not only partnership but also finesse, understanding and, in some instances, a blind eye. Matiullah Khan's men appreciated that they would soon be fighting the war without the big bombs, helicopters, medical evacuation and advanced warfighters to support them. They were reverting to the old ways of fighting, and this was often uncomfortable for the Australians.

'They [Khan's men] had to regain positions of power in their community, and they had to do it by way of dominance,' Porter says. 'They had their own ways of reasserting power. When we are partnering with them we have a responsibility to make sure all our missions are morally and ethically conducted. Things became quite uncomfortable sometimes.'

Greg Barton was commander of Bravo Company on Rot 19. 'It was a tough time for the boys,' he says, 'and a lot of the difficulty was understanding where we were with the Afghans. Some guys got it immediately, some took a bit longer. Cam got it 100 per cent. I have an image etched in my mind of [Jack Ducat] and Cam sitting there talking to the partner force [Afghans], all having a great time.'

Cam and Jack were given split roles on Rot 19. As well as leading their assault teams, they were tasked with mentoring Khan's paramilitary force, which was located adjacent to Camp Russell on the Multi-National Force (MNF) base. It was a role into which both men threw themselves with gusto. Although Cam was more comfortable leading Australian men into battle than he was teaching Afghans relatively elementary warfighting, he understood the importance of what he was being asked to do, and the work stoked his lifelong curiosity in people whose experiences were drastically different from his own.

To hear of Cam asking Afghan soldiers about their home lives and religion reminds me of Cam's mates' many stories about nights out when they momentarily lost him, then discovered him deep in conversation with someone unexpected – a cross-dresser, an elderly couple, a man who appeared to be homeless.

Both Cam and Jack spent a lot more time on the Afghan base than was strictly required. Sometimes they'd be training with the Afghan fighters, but often they'd just be playing volleyball and shooting the shit.

'You like Afghanistan?' an Afghan officer named Usman asked Cam once.

'Yes, mate, it's great,' Cam said, knowing that generous platitudes were an important part of working with the locals.

'You like here in Tarin Kowt?'

'Yep.'

'Okay, there is land near river. I will arrange for you to have. You can live after the war.'

Pause. Longer pause. 'No, mate.'

Jack Ducat tells that story with deadpan glee. No man was closer to Cam in the unit at that time than him, even if they seemed as different as any two men in Bravo. Jack had a flop of hair that seemed to defy grooming standards – it was likely only allowed because he wore it so well. Cam was good-looking but had quite blunt features, while Jack was handsome in the subtle way of an editorial model. When they spoke, they stood either side of the line between subtlety and candour.

So Jack Ducat and Cam Baird were an odd gun-slinging couple, but what they shared was a history of combat efficacy, and an expectation that they would, at some point, both contend to be the regimental sergeant major (RSM) of the unit, the most senior role for a non-commissioned officer in 2 Commando.

'They were such a pair, those two,' says Geoff Goddard, their RSM during Rot 19. 'Such different personalities, but they just worked together – a little bit of yin to each other's yang.'

'Those two really got the partnering thing,' says Porter. 'They fundamentally understood why it was such an important part of the job. There are a lot of differences between Afghans and Australians, but there are similarities, especially if you're a warfighter. The Afghans really resonated with those two, and they really respected that those two were always down there, treating them with respect and dignity.'

Cam and Jack understood that good mentoring in this context had three distinct benefits. The first was building the capacity of the Afghans to fight alongside the Australians in the last missions they would be leading.

This dovetailed into the second benefit, which was building the capacity of the Afghans so they could lead their own operations when the Australians had left. The third was building general rapport and understanding, soldier to soldier. In this aspect, there was an additional, if unstated benefit: perhaps familiarity would mitigate the likelihood of one of the Afghans turning his weapon on the Australians he was fighting alongside.

'Green on blue' or 'insider' attacks were happening with alarming regularity across the country in 2013. One recent incident had seen an Afghan National Army soldier kill three Australian soldiers who had been training him. Sometimes the attacks had been the result of Taliban infiltration, but others were due to more confusing local reasons. If there was a better understanding of what was happening on the Afghan bases, it was felt, the likelihood of these surprise attacks was lessened considerably.

The rules of combat on the ground had changed for this last SOTG rotation. For most of the war, the commandos had been operating under a certain threshold of acceptable danger, but now, with the war coming to an end and the public less accepting of Australian deaths, that threshold had changed. Porter says that, to the best of his abilities, he tried to signal to the guys on the ground what the new standards were – but they were difficult to understand, even for him, and therefore also difficult to codify.

Everyone on the ground knew that the higher-ups wanted the commandos to operate with less exposure, but they were also told they were working towards outcomes that put the Afghans in the best position to take over the fighting after the end of this rotation. (There would be one more SOTG rotation after this, but it would primarily be concerned with extraction and dismantling Camp Russell.) The Taliban tide had to be beaten back enough for the Afghans to take over. That meant operations – dangerous operations. From a foot soldier's perspective, it was contradictory and confusing.

To make matters worse, the soldiers were, for the first time, working with a 50/50 partner ratio, which meant that every time an Aussie gunfighter boarded a chopper, he had to have an Afghan mirror. Strategically, the rule made perfect sense, as the Australians were fast approaching a time when the partner ratio would be 0/100, but incorporating so many relatively inexperienced fighters into a very modern, very complicated battlespace did nothing to lessen the commandos' exposure to risk. One soldier said it was like bringing park footballers into a Premier League game.

'Were we cooking the books? Yeah. A lot of the FEs [force elements] would do it,' Geoff Goddard says. 'We'd have the partner force come with us and stay stationary, and the FE would go do the fighting and then go pick the partner force back up sometimes. The Afghans just didn't want to be in those fights with us. You have to want to fight, and the thing about our guys is they all want to fight. [The Afghans] weren't bad; they were just irrelevant.'

There are stories of the Afghan fighters helping in commando operations, but others in which they were a liability. One Australian soldier told me about a group of Afghans who refused to recover the body of a dead Afghan teammate, which meant an Australian had to head out into gunfire and get him. The commando who told me this story was more perturbed about getting the Afghan's blood all over his brand-new boots than the fact that he had just risked his life.

Another commando told me of an instance in which he and a group of Afghan soldiers discovered a Taliban fighter on a mission. The commando spurred the reluctant Afghans to give chase, and when they caught up with him, not only did they not shoot him, but they gave no indication that they had found him, standing silent as the Australian was shot and wounded.

A further complicating factor for the commandos was that many knew this would likely be the last time they'd see combat. Since Vietnam, the most significant battles experienced by Australian soldiers had been in Afghanistan; when Australia was no longer involved, who knew when the next battle would be? It could be generations. These men were not bloodthirsty but they did love their job. So on Rot 19 the commandos, almost to a man, were doing everything they could do to get on a chopper and participate in gunfights, but it wasn't as easy as it had been in the past.

Not only was the political will of Australians for the conflict waning, it was difficult to get the requisite air assets. Australian special forces had predominantly used foreign Black Hawk and Chinook aircraft to move around southern Afghanistan; now they were one of the few special forces groups still in the country, and the air infrastructure was rapidly disappearing.

Helicopters were found, but were split across an eight-day cycle – four days of choppers for the SASR, then four days for the commandos – but the pilots were conventional pilots, not special forces pilots, so there were tactical constraints that the commandos were not used to.

One was the fact that conventional pilots wouldn't land or take off in contested areas, while special forces pilots would. This frustration was compounded because the warfighters – having worked with special-operations pilots and also in the Russian helos piloted by 'The Expendables' – knew what was possible.

'I saw a CSM arguing with some American pilots, saying, "You need to land here – this is what we fucking need to do," and the American pilots were saying, "We can't, it's too dangerous,"' says Goddard. 'I said, "Mate, what does that say on that aircraft? It fucking says 'US'. This is millions of bucks of American government property. Settle down."'

It was a tense tour, with more stress pressing down on the commandos because of the long lead-time that was required to get a conventional aircraft into the air for a mission. Special forces teams, especially those doing counter-insurgency missions, require the element of surprise in their missions, but the conventional American helicopters needed four days' notice before the commandos could fly.

At a company-wide meeting, Cam, as was often the case, voiced an opinion harboured by all the 2 Commando gunfighters. 'Sir, this four-day mission timeline is killing us,' he told Lieutenant Colonel Porter.

'I remember he gave a pretty compelling case, but it was one of those things,' says Porter. 'It was just a constraint. He accepted that and went on with the job. That rule was incredibly frustrating for me – incredibly frustrating for every commander and soldier working with me.'

Adding to the commandos' frustration, the SASR had been given a dispensation from the rule and were spinning missions up and executing them on the same day. There was little difference between the missions that the SASR and 2 Commando were conducting, but in some political circles the commandos were still perceived as the little brothers.

Then a stunning 'cease ops' order came in from the Chief of Defence. 'All missions out of the wire were cancelled.' This had the potential to completely derail the already fractured relationship between Perth and Holsworthy.

—

On 28 April 2013 some SASR troopers were sent into Zabul Province to hunt a priority target bomb maker codenamed 'Rapier'. They had killed four Taliban, but instead of using biometric scanners to check whether any of the men they'd killed were 'Rapier', they cut the right hands off three of the bodies, taking them back to base. Mutilation like this was a violation of the Geneva Convention, and when the Australian command found out about the incident, all SOTG operations were halted until further notice.

The nature of both the commando and SASR counter-insurgency operations in Afghanistan were layered, in that each mission related to the next, sometimes working further and further up the Taliban command chain. A long combat stoppage could set each FE back significantly, not to mention how the stoppage enraged the foreign elements who were counting on the Aussie gunfighters to do their jobs.

At a SOTG-wide meeting, the commandos' frustration over the SASR fault bubbled over. The 2 Commando's relationship with the Americans had been seriously strained by the 'cease ops' order, and it was jeopardising their last missions in the war. Soldiers from the Sydney-based unit were now openly questioning the professionalism of the Perth men.

Goddard remembers the meeting well. 'Then Cam, in front of everybody, said, "Hey, we're going to fucking support these blokes. We're doing this together – we're all fucking Australian soldiers," pointing to the Australian flag [on his shoulder],' he says. 'That was Cam. He knew exactly what to say. It took all the sting out of the room. The CO of the SASR on the way out said, "Fucking hell, that was impressive."'

The 'cease ops' order lasted another three weeks, and during those weeks, some of the commandos, stuck on base, started to ruminate on the future of the country and the geopolitical role they'd played.

'There was debate, constant debate, on that rotation, about what it was all about, this war,' says Porter. 'There

was a lot of: "This is bullshit; we want to finish the job.'"
The officers had to remind the gunfighters that it was not
their job to finish, nor was this their country.

Some of the commandos have said the frustration
then was not because Afghanistan was an unwinnable
war, but to the contrary – because it *was* winnable. Some
think that Australia could have almost completely pacified
Uruzgan with a brigade-strength deployment, complete with
Australian choppers, artillery, drones and maybe even tanks.

During the 'cease ops', many felt that they had never
actually been sent to Afghanistan to win a war. It raised
thoughts of how many of the Afghan commanders were
conducting the war, fighting for personal power, not necessarily to win. This was a war that the Afghans had been
fighting with their fathers, and would still be fighting with
their sons. Matiullah Khan knew that the possibility of
victory was far smaller than the possibility of enrichment.

At one point, Major General Michael Crane DSC and
Bar AM, Australian Commander in the Middle East,
addressed the SOTG, trying to explain that the current
goal was to create conditions for an appropriate exit and
for Afghan primacy. Many of the men who'd been fighting
in the Taliban-controlled valleys and towns for years felt
he was selling a pipe dream. The soldiers knew what was

going to happen when they left. They had worked with their partner force and Matiullah Khan.

'I'd look at all my guys in combat shirts, ready to go do it, and then at this plump, middle-aged man, who'd never been in combat, telling them how to finish the war,' says the RSM. 'It was funny.'

The commandos never lost their focus and professionalism, but keeping morale high was not easy. It was in this environment that Major General Crane ordered Anzac Day to be commemorated once, by the whole base. This was at odds with what had happened in previous years, with SOTG always conducting its own commemoration. SOTG representatives argued to Major General Crane that they should be able to conduct their own event for the sake of continuity. The request was denied; they decided to do it anyway.

Soldiers from SASR, 2 Commando and the Special Operations Engineer Regiment (SOER), along with some American special forces gunfighters who had been working with the SOTG, came together for a dawn service that included a tribute to all the SOTG members who had been killed in previous rotations. Photographs of the men came up on a screen, while Eddie Vedder – the favourite artist of SASR trooper Sergeant Blaine Diddams, who'd been killed a year earlier in a gunfight with insurgents – was blasted over some speakers.

Afterwards, a piper stood on the roof next to the gathering and played, while photographs of the men came up as the tribute went through the previous 18 rotations. There was a minute's silence, then the ceremony finished with a New Zealand–born SAS trooper doing the haka, shirtless and in war paint, spinning around an old .303 Lee–Enfield rifle, a weapon that was first used by the British in the late 1800s and is still sometimes used by Taliban fighters today.

Later in the day, Geoff Goddard sought out some of his key gunfighters to give them a folder. On each page was a picture of an SOTG member who had been killed. The gesture told the men that they were the keepers of this history. Tell it right, and tell it true.

Cam Baird was given a folder, and over the next three months he augmented the pages with maxims and quotes about leadership and integrity. This was the folder found by Doug and Kaye when they were given Cam's personal effects.

—

That Anzac Day ceremony was, for many of the soldiers, a bookend for their Afghan experience, but almost all wanted to get into the fight again the next day. They were there and they wanted to fight right up until that last flight out of Tarin Kowt. Greyhounds run, eagles fly, commandos fight. There would only be a few more significant battles after Anzac Day, the last being the biggest, and the most tragic.

After that final mission, the guys were only a few weeks from leaving Afghanistan for good. Major General Crane approached Geoff Goddard. 'I can't believe you're still getting guys killed out here,' he said.

Enraged, the enlisted man turned to the general and decided to speak his mind – fuck the consequences. 'That's your fault,' he said. 'Your fault and Canberra's fault. We can go home tomorrow, but when we're here we fight. That's our fucking job.'

CHAPTER FIFTEEN

THE ROLLING THUNDER

'Just fucking keep your head down, mate.'

TOM PORTER

TARIN KOWT, AFGHANISTAN
KHOD VALLEY, AFGHANISTAN
22 JUNE 2013

Cameron Baird woke tired but happy. He was excited –
there were going to be gunfights today.

It would have been perhaps 4 a.m. when Cam Baird
got out of his cot, having climbed into bed only a few
hours earlier. He'd been debriefing command about the
previous day's operation, an attack on a nearby valley.
It had included a fake exfiltration – helos coming in and
loitering just long enough for the Taliban to believe that

the Australians had left, before the commandos conducted a surprise second attack.

The mission had been a good one, but it had only been an amuse-bouche, planned to excite and identify Taliban command and control elements, which, it was hoped, would flock into the nearby Khod Valley, a centre of narcotics activity, a Taliban stronghold and an area of great strategic importance. Today's mission would be to neutralise those elements.

The insurgency had slowly been consolidating its power in the valley for months, with intel surmising that, at some point after the coalition withdrawal, the Taliban would use the Khod as a supply line for an assault on Tarin Kowt. Over several weeks the enemy had become increasingly bold in their actions in and around the valley, with the Taliban recently overrunning two police check-points the Australians had set up for Matiullah Khan, murdering those manning them. The mission today was to flush through the Khod, killing or detaining any Taliban fighters. The hope was that the commandos would find the commanders, the *real* Taliban.

Cam's first stop that morning was the command centre at Tarin Kowt, where he checked in on how Quebec, Bravo's other platoon, was faring. The day before, when Cam's platoon, Romeo, had been conducting their attack and fake exfiltration, Quebec was already fighting in the Khod Valley.

Quebec had inserted just to the south of a small cluster of compounds called Ghawchak Village. They'd initiated some fighting; multiple enemy and one friendly Afghan had been killed. As per the plan, they had pulled back from the valley and set up a cordon of snipers and mortars on the high ground. The hope was that more Taliban would rush into the valley, ready to engage in what they thought was a single-fronted battle.

Cam and the Romeo assault teams would insert a few kilometres away from the cordon and rush down the valley, driving the enemy fighters into Quebec's bombs and bullets. Romeo would be a blitzkrieg, a hurricane; it was Cam Baird's type of mission.

'We changed our way of doing things at the end,' says Santi Sambara. 'A lot of the insurgency thought there was no point in getting killed by us now, so the Taliban would shoot at you and, if you'd lose him in the trees or hills or something, he'd just put his weapon down and become a friendly again. We found the best thing for us was to overwhelm them quickly, and not give them the opportunity to transition. That's what Cam was so good at, just getting off the chopper and fucking running into battle, with his team behind.'

In the command centre, Cam would have watched live footage from an unmanned aerial vehicle (UAV) circling the valley, looking for features that he and his team could exploit or should be wary of. While in the command centre it's likely he also checked in with one or more of the intelligence officers, who were monitoring enemy communications chatter and getting direct information from the platoon on the ground.

Happy in the knowledge that not only were things in hand, there was also likely going to be a good amount of fighting that day, Cam went to the base gym, where, as he always did, he weighed himself. Cam had calculated that his optimal combat weight was 100 kilograms, so he tried to keep at that weight, on the dot.

The Camp Russell gym was a popular place, but at this early hour, and with one platoon outside the wire and a second prepping to fly, Cam met only one other man, Geoff Goddard, who was toiling away on the treadmill.

'Big day, Cam?' Goddard asked.

'Oh, yeah, it's going to be awesome, sir, awesome,' he replied.

Cam did 30 or 40 minutes of weights, then a light cardio workout, before hitting the showers. By this time the rest of his platoon were starting their day.

Music always blasted out of the shower block before ops, and that morning Dead Letter Circus, an alt-rock outfit from Brisbane, was the band of choice. Double-kick drums and bass thrummed and guitars soared below a controlled scream.

Stay here ignorant forever now
Change and grow toward a better now
Escape is over for the ever now
Survive this will no one
Will no one?

Cam jumped into his combat gear and, with weapons, ammo, grenades and radio collected, headed for the flight line.

All the chalks were lined up and ready to pile into two fat-bellied Chinook helicopters, with Cam at the back of the queue. Last in the helicopter and first out – that was Bairdy's way.

One officer told of sitting in the command centre earlier on that rotation, watching a helicopter disgorge men into a landing zone. As they filed out, ground fire started peppering the aircraft. This officer watched one solitary man sprint towards the attackers, with a group of soldiers attempting to keep up. The officer had no doubt who the streaking blip on the screen was.

A few weeks earlier, Lieutenant Colonel Tom Porter had actually warned Cam about the pace at which he came out of the helicopter. It wasn't an order, or even really advice from a superior, just concern from a mate. 'Just fucking keep your head down, mate,' he had said.

'Yep, sir, no worries.'

Now Cam stretched as he waited to get in the chopper and did little shuffle-step sprints, as though he was about to run onto the football field. As the men piled into the two Chinooks that would take Romeo towards the fight, there was a sense of immense excitement. There were perhaps no more excited soldiers than Jack and Cam, the commandos in charge of the two assault teams that would be bum-rushing the Taliban up into the cordon. Cam's legs vibrated like a bass string. He caught Jack's gaze and let out a whoop. His mate smiled.

The first Chinook heading into the valley would have the bulk of the door-kickers – including Cam and Jack and their teams. In the second chopper was a grab bag of Matiullah Khan's PRC fighters and another assault team, commanded by Tim Stanton, with Santi Sambara behind him.

Santi had been in the Army for almost a decade now, but as he jumped out of the chopper in the Khod Valley he still looked like a kid. He was a multiple-tour vet, and a father – he had moved from Alpha Company to Bravo so his Afghanistan rotations wouldn't always coincide with his kid's birthday – but he just had one of those youthful faces.

As soon as the second chopper touched down, there was work to do. Jack's and Cam's teams ran ahead, and shortly after touching down Santi saw movement on the hills above them – squirters running away from Cam and Jack, most likely. Santi radioed their positions to command, who could decide whether they needed some Hellfire or .50-calibre attention.

As Santi and his team started clearing the compounds that Cam's and Jack's teams had already swept through, one of his interpreters told him what the Taliban were saying on the radio: they weren't cutting and running today; they were digging in. This was a little unusual, but not completely unexpected. The Taliban had become intermittently emboldened in recent months. They were testing the Australians' resolve.

Santi and his Afghan PRC fighters met with little resistance as they cleared the compounds through which the assault had stormed. Every so often the radio would tell them about the fighting that was happening ahead of them. Cam had been especially busy.

'He was just running a tally that day,' Santi remembers. 'He'd come over the radio and it'd be like, "I've got a couple of guys with a machine gun," or, "I see some dudes moving into a cave complex."' After a call like that, 7.62 mm and 5.56 mm gunfire would echo down the valley. 'Next thing would be Cam popping up on the radio saying, "Got 'em." It was awesome – they'd just been rolling dudes up.'

As they moved further into the valley, Santi started having issues with his communications equipment – perhaps there was interference because of the iron ore in the ground, which was also affecting the commandos' compasses.

More gunfire rattled down the valley, and then more. There was a flurry of messages back and forth, but Santi only snatched parts of them here and there. He tried to patch them into a complete picture but it was difficult. What he did know for sure was that one of the Australians had been shot. He didn't know who was down, but he could tell that efforts were being made to get to him.

Cam popped up on Tim's radio. He and his team were moving towards the downed man.

'I actually wasn't too worried,' says Greg Barton, who was in a command position above the valley. 'Everyone was still moving, and Cam and his team [were] moving to the casualty. All good.'

Santi and his team continued to clear the compounds, until a relentless tempest of gunfire came rattling down the valley. 'All of a sudden the whole place just went nuts,' he says. 'We were three or four hundred metres away from it, but we could tell from the rate of fire that it was just an epic shitfight. You couldn't even differentiate between our guys' [gunfire] and theirs – it was just constant shooting and explosions.'

Santi and Tim were waiting for the Afghans, who'd been clearing behind them, when the cacophony started. They looked at each other and, without a word, sprinted down the valley, towards the village. They might have received a call to move but it wasn't needed.

Santi ran towards the Ghawchak Village wall. He suspected the wall separated him from the path where the Australian casualty had been sustained. When Santi got to the wall, he braced it with two hands, ready to vault over it, before one of the other Aussies, who'd been pushing forward and to his left, yelled and held up a hand, indicating he should stop. After a pause, some 5.56 mm rounds rang out. When Santi peeked his head over the wall, he found, almost directly below him, a dead Taliban fighter. Good work, flank.

Near the dead man the Australians found a mat, shoes and an AK-47, bundled around a corner. It was an ambush position, quite possibly where the shooter of the first casualty had been hiding. Even though the Australians would have to be a little warier in their advance, Santi and Tim were keen to get to the gunfire as soon as possible. It was still ringing out, barely ceasing.

The PRC fighters arrived and Santi told them they would be pushing on towards the fight. The rate of fire up the valley increased even more. The cracks of shots and booms of grenades bounced around the compound walls. The Afghans wanted nothing to do with it, but the Australians tried to urge them on.

'The Afghans kept saying, "Five minutes, five minutes – wait five minutes,"' remembers Santi, 'and I said, "No, not five minutes, now. Now!"'

While Santi argued with the Afghans, the other Australians from his team moved up, and soon he was left with just the PRC troops and one Aussie machine-gunner. Even though they weren't technically under his command, Santi tried ordering them to move on. They wouldn't budge. Then one of the Afghans started firing his AK-47 into an adjacent double-storey compound about ten metres away.

'Talib! Talib!' he said, pointing towards where he'd been firing.

Santi sent one of the Aussie gunners to the top of a nearby building for overwatch, planning to breach the compound with his Afghan fighters. Once again, they flatly refused to advance. They were spooked.

'Come, come, I need help,' said Santi, motioning and pointing towards the compound door. No dice. They were frozen. Fearing an ambush that could flank those moving to the casualty, Santi knew he had to clear that compound immediately – and that he'd have to do it on his own.

'I was getting nervous,' he says. 'Things were getting really heightened. I pulled one of my grenades out and was about to throw it over the wall before going in, but something in my mind said, "Don't . . . don't."'

Santi busted through the compound door and found a group of terrified women and children. He felt momentary relief – he could have killed them all.

With his back against a wall, Santi started calling people out of the compound's rooms. Perhaps a dozen men warily emerged. None were armed, but he was concerned they might not stay that way if they realised they were facing just one commando. 'I really started shitting myself,' he says.

Then, to Santi's immense relief, the PRC fighters started entering the compound. He told them to clear the rooms and secure the men. As they did, he moved back to his machine-gunner's position to get a report on the situation. When he got to the roof, he saw a group carrying a stretcher. On it was a man lying still, covered by a cloth, with multi-cam pants and boots sticking out.

'I thought it was a terp [interpreter] that had been killed, and I was wondering what an interpreter was doing up front,' he says. 'Then I realised it wasn't a terp – I could tell who it was. I couldn't see anything identifying, but I could just fucking tell who it was.'

CHAPTER SIXTEEN

HAPPINESS IS A WARM GUN

'You all good to keep pushing forward?'

CAMERON BAIRD

KHOD VALLEY, AFGHANISTAN
22 JUNE 2013

Jack Ducat and Cam Baird had fought this war, shoulder to shoulder, almost from post to post. Jack had been with Cam on the raid in Chenartu, through the Kajaki job, the start of helo ops, on the DEA rotations and now, here.

The responsibilities and skills of the two men had progressed in concert throughout the war, and now they were the pair responsible for the teams that would be sweeping through a notorious area of enemy control, facing Taliban fighters who had been deliberately agitated.

More than that, they were the closest of mates, sharing a bond that's hard to emulate outside the realm of conflict. In exactly a year's time, Jack would be holding his day-old first-born in his arms, having given the child the middle name Cameron in tribute to his brother in arms. That day, however, Jack was there to fight.

Both Jack's and Cam's teams had expected resistance, and resistance they found, and fairly quickly. As per the assault plan, both teams were out of the helo quickly, with Jack's pushing up to the river by the village. There they started taking in rounds.

Moving quickly to the river after coming out of the choppers had become standard procedure for the commandos. The Taliban regularly stored their weapons at the river, away from their buildings, so that if they were surprised by coalition soldiers in their homes they could easily feign innocence.

Often the race to the river indicated what kind of day the commandos were going to have. If the Taliban melted away as the Aussies approached, it was most likely a quiet day. If they grabbed their guns and fired back, it was on. On this day, it was well and truly on.

'At the river there was a pretty decent rate of fire,' Jack says. 'We pushed them to the other side.'

279

The two teams split up. Cam's pushed into the compound cluster, while Jack and his team set up in a clearing, ready to interdict. It didn't take long for Cam to start pushing squirters towards Jack and his team, who killed them one by one. A few other fighters came in from the high ground; they were killed quickly too.

'We didn't expect that many guys,' says Jack. 'We expected to push up to the crew down at the block, but we had some pretty big contacts and big numbers of enemy KIA straightaway. It wasn't anything we couldn't handle, though.'

When they had some breathing space, Jack and Cam met up to talk about what to do next. Some intel came in: the Taliban were planning to set up an ambush at a nearby grove of plum trees.

'What do you wanna do?' Jack asked Cam.

'Let's keep going.'

'Sweet.'

It was unusual for commandos to grab a Taliban commander when they dropped into a village, but the fact that there were so many fighters willing to stand and fight indicated that there might be a command element nearby. If they scattered this ambush and pushed more guys into the block, maybe they'd catch some high-value targets. Both teams would work as a long, extended cordon. If there were any Taliban on the valley floor, they were going to be found.

An enemy on the high ridge, above Jack's team, started shooting at the commandos. Jack and his guys stopped to engage him, while Cam's team pushed on to where the Taliban had said they were going to try to spring an ambush.

After the fighter on the high ground had been killed, Jack's team swung back towards the compound cluster. Soon they could hear gunshots from where Cam's team had been, but from the rate of fire they could tell that things were in hand. Cam came back on comms: the wannabe ambushers were either dead or had scarpered.

The comms crackled again. It was an intel update: a few Taliban had amassed at the compound cemetery a little further ahead on the high ground.

Cam and Jack had a quick powwow over the radio.

'You all good to keep pushing forward?' Cam asked.

'Yep, sweet,' Jack responded.

The teams would consolidate again at the cemetery.

Jack's men funnelled through a built-up area. Jack led the way, and found himself in a corridor with high walls either side. A Taliban with a gun popped up in front of him, running from right to left. He was likely trying to make it to a place where he could set an ambush. Jack already had his rifle at his shoulder and squeezed off a couple of rounds. The man dropped.

Jack ran over to administer the kill shots, but as he put two more rounds into the bloke, bullets smashed into the wall above him. He turned to see where the fire had come from and immediately another burst came in. Some of the rounds were low, some high, but one 7.62 mm round crashed into Jack's chest plate and another into his femur, shattering it. He tumbled into the dust.

Jack's guys instantly ran forward, with heavy gunfire and grenades, to where the rounds had come from. Meanwhile, Jack had propped himself up and was trying to drag himself to cover. It was slow going until one of his guys stopped firing and dragged his team leader to a doorway, and then applied a pressure bandage to his wound.

After inspecting the wound, the medic treating Jack sent a general call out over the comms: '4-Key, Cat A.'

4-Key was Jack's designation in the battle. Category A meant he needed to get medical treatment in the next hour – or he was either losing a limb or his life.

Cam called over the radio: he was coming to his mate, ASAP.

As one of the other commandos explained, Jack had just enough medical knowledge to get himself in trouble. He started jamming up the comms channel, explaining how he should be treated and extracted. Then a rising crescendo of gunfire and explosion started just east of his position, which silenced him momentarily. This was one hell of a fight.

A few of Jack's team wanted to prepare him for extraction, but Jack was on the comms again, trying to figure out what was happening just a couple of walls away. One team member says he was thinking about ripping the earpiece out of his team leader's ear. Jack was likely going into shock, and in no position to add anything else to this battle. He was a complication now, not a contributor. Jack had to calm down and wait to be helped.

The rate of fire to his east rose, and then rose again. Jack tried to follow the fight on the comms, but couldn't always hear what was being said over the heavy gunfire. Then he heard something distinct. Something he could scarcely believe. 'You fucking what?' Jack yelled over the comms.

His earpiece was torn out. *One problem at a time, mate.*

But they had all heard the casualty call.

'3-Key, KIA.'

CHAPTER SEVENTEEN

MEMENTO MORI

'Be ready for room-floor combat.'

CAMERON BAIRD

KHOD VALLEY, AFGHANISTAN
22 JUNE 2013

Jeremy 'Jez' Thorne was behind Cameron Baird's shoulder for most of his last mission. In fact, Jez was behind Cam for most of his last rotation. He was a junior member of the team, but had already proven himself a fearsome, reliable and aggressive fighter. Just the type Cam liked in his chalk.

Jez came from a military family stretching back all the way to the Boer War. He had great-uncles who had fought at Gallipoli, a grandfather who was part of the RAAF, a father who was in the Ordnance Corps, and two older brothers serving when he left school, one a cavalry sergeant and the other, Brandon, a commando.

After dropping out of school in Year 11, Jez applied for a panelbeating apprenticeship and for the Army. The Army called first and, after basic training, he became an infantryman. Jez did one deployment to Afghanistan with 1RAR. He was happy to get over, but didn't come back with stories like the ones his commando brother told him. 'When you're an infantry soldier you want to be in the thick of it, in the heat of battle, but that trip was pretty much babysitting,' he says.

Jez decided to try for special forces selection one Anzac Day, when Brandon invited him to meet his workmates. 'We were drinking at Customs House,' he says, 'and my brother was like, "You gotta meet this dude Cam Baird." I was like that groupie kid, hanging on. They had hot girlfriends and a big chest of gongs – they were the shit.'

Brandon didn't tell his little brother anything specific about selection, but said that if he could do it, then Jez could too. In the event, Jez didn't just pass selection, he excelled. Brandon was impressed, and so were Jack Ducat and Cam Baird.

Bravo Company had very smartly offered themselves up to help with the selection courses, and it was there that the team commanders started to make notes about who they might want to take on in their teams. When Jez came up in the reinforcement cycle, Jack helped him into Bravo, where he ended up as junior under Cam. This was true of all the men in Cam's and Jack's chalks – they'd all been watched since selection.

For a junior door-kicker, being behind Cam or Jack was pretty much the most desirable position to be in. 'They all wanted to be in Cam's team, because they knew that Cam would get them into the fighting,' says Geoff Goddard.

On 22 June 2013, that was certainly the truth.

———

It was Jez's job to get out of the chopper as quickly as Cameron Baird. There were six commandos in the chalk led by Baird, with a special forces engineer and interpreter attached, as well as a few of Matiullah Khan's men.

Jez was the team's designated medic, but with the team scout having been shot a few weeks earlier, he was also tasked with pathfinding. As the load door of the Chinook opened, Jez was scanning the ground below, looking for patterns of life.

The team split up for the commandos' regular tactical advance, with the Aussies working in pairs. As Jez advanced, he had a couple of partner force guys following. When they saw some fighting-aged males in the distance, the Afghans opened up.

Cam saw some potential threats across the shallow river they would be following. The original assault plan hadn't called for them to cross the river, but during the planning stage Cam had told his platoon commander, Greg Barton, that he saw the area as a potential flank security issue. Now he took a couple of men with him across the river and started engaging a group of between six and ten armed men. Some were killed, while others melted away. When Cam got on the radio and checked in with Barton, who was part of a command element on the high side of one of the valley walls, his platoon commander smiled. *Fair play, Cam*, he thought.

Cam and his group crossed back over and the chalk pushed ahead. The fight was on now, and the enemy communications started to become more frequent and excited. The interpreter was telling the Australians what was being said – the normal shit about 'bringing the big ones up' and 'killing the infidels'.

Snipers above observed some men digging up a cache of weapons, so Cam's team now split back into their pairs. Two commandos were engaged by a PK machine gun, as well as an AK-47 and an old bolt-action rifle. These were likely the men who hoped to ambush Cam and his team, but they were killed or scattered when the Australians started firing back.

Nearby was a cave in the valley wall that had been identified as a potentially hazardous firing point, so before moving on Cam decided they should head up and make sure there were no potential threats. The spot was deserted, allowing the assault team a moment of respite.

They went back to the point where they had killed the would-be ambushers, seized their weapons and did biometric scans of the corpses. In a moment that can scarcely be understood by those unfamiliar with the Afghan conflict, some children appeared, looking for gifts. The commandos had some sweets and colouring books for times just like this; after shedding themselves of their presents, they pushed on.

As they moved forward, a call came in from the overwatch position. The sniper team had observed some Taliban fighters moving to the cave the guys had just cleared. Cam and his team held position while the snipers got clean shots on the enemy trying to get to firing positions. After the kill shots had all rung out, the Australians pushed further along the valley.

Cam caught up with Jack on the radio. There was chatter on the radio about the Taliban planning an ambush at the cemetery, but the Taliban always talked a big game. Cam and Jack decided to push ahead. Things were going well. They were ripping through this valley.

The teams split. Jack and his guys moved deep into Ghawchak Village proper, while Cam's team moved alongside, flanking. Then Cam and Jez heard the echo of gunfire from the village – the report and echo of the shots bouncing through the alleys and walls of the compound. There was more gunfire, and then more.

'Be ready for room-floor combat,' Cam said to Jez, a huge grin on his face.

Room-floor combat was the toughest fighting: getting through each room, each nook and cranny of these ancient, inscrutable mud-brick complexes. It was something Cam often said when the fighting was going to become hard and complicated.

'Man, he loved that shit,' recalls Jez.

The call came in over the radio: 4-Key was 'Cat A'. Jack was down. Cam had to get to his best mate, and the commandos who loved to play offence were now on the defensive.

Cam and his team ran into the village and towards Jack as quickly as they could, which wasn't particularly fast in the warren of walls, huts and compounds. Rooms and nooks still had to be cleared; flanks and rears had to be protected; corners had to be approached with trepidation.

Jez describes what happened next: 'Bairdy was up front. I was cleaning a hole in the wall (there were many keyholes in these ancient walls, perfect for taking pot shots) and I heard this burst of fire from the rear.'

The last commando of the group had been doing rear security, looking backwards as the team moved forward. After the group had passed a relatively large structure – which may have been serving as a place of worship, a meeting hall or both – he saw the long, distinctive barrel of a PK machine gun.

The workhorse heavy weapon of the Soviet Army, the Pulemyot Kalashnikov can fire hundreds of rounds a minute; in the confines of a passageway like the one that the commandos were walking through, it could have dropped them all in moments. As soon as the rear security commando saw the rifle, he started firing.

They all rushed to the fire, and the target designation was shouted in typical Aussie style: 'We got one fucking cunt in here!'

The fire had come from the doorway of an antechamber. It led to a larger room, and it was here the PK gunner had fled. There were two doorways to the antechamber, on opposite sides of the space. Half of Cam's chalk stacked up against the doorway where the gun had been seen, while the other half, including Cam, moved around to the other side.

On the way, Cam saw a Taliban fighter moving to the sound of the gunfire. The Afghan was dead before he could raise his weapon.

When the two teams were stacked up, they started one of their close-quarters drills, with one man shooting into the doorway while his partner posted fragmentation grenades.

'We'd shoot, they'd shoot, we'd shoot, they'd shoot, we throw a frag into their door and it's quiet and we hope those cunts are dead,' says Jez. 'Then they start lighting us up again.'

Cam moved around to Jez's door, using the warning designation – which is basically shouting out a specific word previously agreed upon to notify the other commandos that a friendly was approaching. When he got there, Jez asked what the play was. They had no idea how many Taliban were in the room; all they knew was that at least one was still alive and armed. There were three options available: bypass the room, call in ordnance from an air asset, or deal with the situation there and then.

In Cam's mind there would have been no choice. Bypassing a PK machine gun like that would have been leaving themselves and Jack's team vulnerable to a potentially disastrous re-engagement. Calling in a drone strike in such a built-up area was also a non-starter. This situation had to be dealt with now, and Cam's team would have to do it.

—

The commandos had been posting frag grenades from outside the antechamber with no apparent effect, but perhaps if they posted from inside it might be different. The boys had no sense of the internal configuration of the ancient room – the enemy might be hiding behind internal walls or cover – but if they could peg a grenade in there, surely they had a better chance of success.

'Mate, should I do it?' Jez asked Cam, holding up his last frag grenade. The commandos had been fighting all morning, and were getting low on ammunition.

'Yeah, do it,' Cam said. 'On me,' he yelled, moving into the antechamber and firing his M4 rifle at the door. Jez followed and posted his last grenade deep into the room.

There was momentary quiet. 'Let the dust settle!' Cam yelled to his boys. The direct sunlight wasn't working in the Aussies' favour. Every grenade had kicked up a small storm of dust, and when they attacked the door they were staring into shades of darkness, while the Taliban inside were seeing silhouettes in the doorway, easy targets.

There was some hurried conversation among the commandos about how to assault this position. They had some demolition charges, as well as a 'snip', a small charge for breaching doors. Perhaps they could blow a hole in one of the walls and flank these fuckers. More fire came from the doorway, with bullets slamming into the ground and doorway around the commandos. It seemed the enemy were now using keyholes around the door, which had been created by the shrapnel from the Australian grenades. The situation was becoming even less stable.

There was no time to set up a breach. There was a lot of firepower in that compound, and it needed to be silenced – now. The site where Jack was being treated had to be secured immediately.

'Righto,' Cam said, pushing into the antechamber and towards the doorway.

'Normally we say "On me" and "On you" as we move,' says Jez, 'but when you're in a battle like that, you've got so much SA [situational awareness], you know exactly what to do.' He followed, covering his team commander's advance. 'We didn't get much further, probably shorter than the last time. There must have been a sweet spot where the sun hit us, and then they started blasting.'

Cam was returning fire in a gunfight at a range of perhaps three or four metres. Then he had a stoppage on his M4, so he and Jez had to peel back out of the antechamber.

Cam ejected a cartridge and checked either side of his rifle for damage. He saw none. He changed magazines and prepared for another assault. This was possibly a fatal decision. It's likely that, in the previous exchange, a Taliban bullet had hit the barrel of Cam's rifle, denting the flash eliminator at the end of his gun. That structural issue would have affected his weapon's ability to 'cycle', likely causing the previous stoppage. As his training dictated, Cam had checked his weapon, and he had found no obvious problems.

Jez was almost out of ammunition for his M4. 'Throw us the RPK,' he said to their interpreter. The Russian RPK rifle had been taken from a Taliban fighter killed earlier. Jez had used this rifle many times before, mostly while training the Afghan fighters, who by now had all melted away.

Cam's mood was sanguine. He likely felt the urgency of the moment, but was confident in his own abilities, and in the capacity of the men around him. These men, whom he had helped mould into fighters, would no more hesitate in the face of death than he would.

'Two seconds earlier he was being fucking lit up,' Jez recalls, 'and now he was cool as shit, making sure everyone was all good. That was Cam.'

Cameron Baird had spent his life searching for a moment that was made for his capacity for action, leadership and courage. He'd built that capacity to the highest of standards, and pulled his team to a commensurate position by word and action. Here, at the end of his life, he was where he had always wanted to be: on the bloody edge of what a gunfighter could do, with brothers he trusted completely.

'He'd been a huge mentor for me on that trip,' says Jez. 'We fight in pairs, and in heaps of gunfights it had been the two of us. I always tried to work with Cam because he was always in the thick of the fight. I was really inspired by Cam. I was just feeling the morale and the aggression of the moment and I went for it. He's looked at me and sees I'm about to make entry so he followed behind me.'

Jez, one of Cam's protégés, hand-picked from selection and reinforcement, charged towards the door with his Russian weapon raised. Cam moved in concert, his M4 covering the junior soldier, who he'd trained to be able to both follow and initiate.

In that moment, Cam was more than 15 000 kilometres away from the clipped grass of Gladstone Park and the busy streets of south-eastern Sydney. He was a world away from his mother and father, who were preparing dinner, and from his brother, who was helping Cam's nephews with their homework. He was a world away from his mates, who were watching footy at the pub, and from a girlfriend who was putting her clothes into the drawers at his house.

As he attacked the door, though, Cam would have had no thoughts of home. He was focused only on what was in front of him: an injured mate, a team to command, an enemy armed to the teeth. A commando dedicates himself to his brother operators before all else. This dedication, for Cameron Baird, was absolute.

Cam charged at the door and started firing. He loosed off a few rounds, which slammed into the body of one of the enemy fighters inside, before his rifle became inert. There was pressure on the trigger and rounds in the clip, but nothing coming from the barrel. It was the dead man's pull. A burst of PK machine-gun fire came from the doorway: one bullet hit just above Cam's chest plate, and another just below his right eye.

Cameron Baird was dead.

CHAPTER EIGHTEEN

THE SETTLED DUST

'It is now time to sheath your dagger.'

A SOTG OFFICER, SPEAKING AT THE RAMP CEREMONY FOR CAMERON BAIRD

One commando told me that he wishes he'd gone out the way Cam did. 'Gun up, charging at the enemy on pretty much the last mission of the last rotation. That's how to do it,' he said.

Another one said: 'It's hard to get excited about anything after you've hunted men.' Yet another commando, a father of two children, told me he would happily have kept fighting in Afghanistan until his body fell apart.

Two men I interviewed told me they had been hospitalised for depression and symptoms of post-traumatic stress disorder. A few others have told me of problems commensurate with PTSD.

The day after I sent the first draft of this book to the publisher, Eddie Robertson sent me a message asking if I had interviewed Ian 'Turns' Turner, a young father and close friend of Cam's. I had, out at Holsworthy Barracks. I'd found him a very personable bloke, willing to answer any question.

He'd been most voluble when talking about the work the commandos had done in the Kajaki Fan, saying that the fighting there had been some of the most favourable.

Ian and I spoke on Facebook a few weeks afterwards, and he told me that images of that Kajaki job just wouldn't leave his mind. He said he rarely thought about the rotations after the Kajaki job, which included missions that were more kinetic and violent, but that job in Helmand simply stayed in his thoughts.

Ian said he'd just gotten out of hospital. 'The price of chasing the action too long,' he said.

We spoke a little about PTSD and he said this: 'I feel like it comes in waves. Every now and again it just hits you. Other times it doesn't even bother you.'

At the end of our chat Ian said he was feeling much better.

'It's all good, mate.'

I told Eddie that I had interviewed Turns. He told me that Ian had just taken his own life.

War is tragic. War is exhilarating. War is also a drug.

In Afghanistan, the commandos saw the frozen faces of death. They saw bullets smash into bodies and faces, punching holes and sometimes blowing off fingers and jaws. They saw grenade fragments burrow into stomachs, livers and hearts. They saw Hellfire and Javelin missiles scatter body parts, fleshy and red, across dusty fields.

They saw death many times over, with an internal estimate suggesting Australian forces had killed 6000 Afghans during the war. The commandos saw death, and then they went back to Sydney. They repainted spare rooms and shopped for ripe avocados. They took their kids to school. They collected their wives' cars from the mechanics' garages. Through their eyes they saw images of suburban life. In their minds they saw Afghanistan. They saw triumph and success: an enemy dead, an existential threat resolved. They saw a commando's greatest tragedy, a brother fallen.

The first person to know that Cameron Baird had been killed was Jez Thorne. While firing his RPK into the compound door, Jez too had a stoppage. He retreated out of the antechamber and back to cover, as Cam was still sending rounds into the room. With rounds smashing into the ground and walls around him, blasting pieces of mud-brick into his face, Jez resolved the stoppage in his rifle and put another mag in. He moved up to the doorway, ready to conduct a fourth assault with his team commander. Jez joined the chorus of commandos telling each other where they were.

One of the other commandos peered into the antechamber and, through the dust and debris, saw Australian boots and multi-cam pants. One of their number was lying on the ground, just outside the door.

'Someone's down!' he yelled.

When Jez had moved back to cover, he had assumed Cam had done the same, but through an entrance on the other side of the antechamber. Now he realised Cam hadn't made it. 'Fuck, it's Bairdy!' he yelled out.

Cam was unresponsive, but his team had no idea what his injuries were. They had to get to him. Jez threw the RPK to the engineer, picked up his M4 and slapped in his last magazine.

'I was pretty fucking on then,' he remembers. 'The other blokes are still getting lit up from the doorway and Cam's down, and we just wanted to fucking get him out.'

Another junior gunfighter in Cam's team yelled that he had one grenade left and that he was going to post it as far as he could into the room. Jez started laying down covering fire as the man ran at the door, closer and closer until it looked as though he was going to run straight through it. 'He practically could have grabbed one of the dudes when he threw. Heaps brave,' says Jez.

The frag exploded deep inside the room. Jez, disoriented from the concussion of the grenades, near-deaf from the relentless, close-quarters gunfire and near-blind from the dust, charged into the antechamber while firing his weapon. Through the haze he saw the shoulder strap of Cam's webbing. He grabbed it and dragged his giant mate out of harm's way. But when he looked down at Cam's wounds, he knew instantly there was no way of surviving them. 'I could see Bairdy was dead,' he says, 'and I had a fuckin' weak moment, mate.'

Jez took Baird's ammo and divided it up between his team. A minute later, part of Tim Stanton's team turned up, relatively flush with supplies. They filled the room with grenades and gunfire, and finally the Taliban guns fell silent. Inside they found six dead Afghans, most riddled with shrapnel wounds, and a huge cache of small arms, machine guns and rockets.

From the moment Cameron Baird started moving to his injured best mate till the moment he was shot dead had been no more than a few minutes – perhaps even less than two – but his quick actions and those of his team had demonstrated extreme bravery, sacrifice and professionalism. Cometh the hour, cometh the men. Those scant minutes of frantic action were a lifetime in the making.

—

News of Cameron Baird's death spread.

First it reached Greg Barton, who was in a command position above the battle.

'3-Key, KIA,' was the call over the radio.

'Get fucked,' was Barton's reaction. Later, he said that the moment he learned Australians had run towards gunfire to help a wounded mate was one of the most profound experiences of his life. Before Barton could feel human concern, however, he had to address the tactical concerns. He ordered the Quick Response Force to get in their helicopter and go wheels up. The SASR element on base was also stood to.

'I can't explain the feeling that goes through everyone when a team commander goes down,' he says.

Both forces were stood down shortly afterwards. This battle was over, and the medivac birds reached the men without any issue.

Geoff Goddard, who, just a few hours earlier, had been in the gym with Cam, met the medical choppers as they came into the base. The last intelligence he'd been given was that both Cam and Jack had been killed. When Jack came in alive with a leg wound, Goddard began to hope that Cam, too, would touch down alive. But when he saw Cam, his face covered in a combat wrap, and his wrists and ankles zip-tied, he knew his star junior NCO was lost.

Goddard and Jez Thorne, who had been escorting his team commander since his death, helped put Cam's body in a US Humvee and drove with him to the medical building. In the quiet, sterilised environment, the blood and dirt of battle on their uniforms seemed out of place. So too their weapons. Jez was pacing manically – in the manner, Goddard says, of a lion in a cage waiting to be fed.

Goddard called Jez over. He took the younger man's hand and the pair started cleaning the blood from Cam's face. They took Cam's webbing off and removed the items from his pouches. They popped the mag out of his M4 and checked the chamber of his M203 grenade launcher. Inside was a 'gold top' round – Cam's munition of choice. They removed it and placed it on the bench. Next to it they rested Cam's rifle. The M4 was an artefact now, destined to be behind glass at the Australian War Memorial in Canberra, where it could be contemplated by schoolkids and tourists.

Jez started to settle, just a little. The battle was over. The war was over. It was all over.

Later, as Cam's body was loaded onto a C-130 for transportation back to Australia, a ramp ceremony was conducted. Jeremy Thorne read out a quote from the Native American warrior poet Tecumseh. It's a special forces staple, but especially fitting for Cam Baird.

> Give thanks to the joy of living. If you see no reason to give thanks, then the fault lies only in yourself. When it comes your time to die, be not like those whose hearts are full with fear of death. Sing your death song proudly, and die like a warrior going home.

—

News of Cam's death now travelled to Canberra, and to Holsworthy, and then to Queensland.

Lieutenant Colonel Tom Porter had flown to Yungaburra, in the Cairns hinterland, for the opening of the Avenue of Honour, a memorial in tribute to all Australians killed in Afghanistan, willed into existence by the parents of commando Ben Chuck, who had lived in the region. Ben had died in the 2010 helicopter crash that had also taken the lives of Scott Palmer and Tim Aplin.

Standing next to a group of politicians, including Prime Minister Julia Gillard and Opposition Leader Tony Abbott, Porter listened as the names of all those killed in Afghanistan were read out. Afterwards, he waited for the crowds to leave, walked to the memorial and placed a unit coin on the base of the monument, below the double-diamond commando insignia.

Respectfully he touched each name. *Fuck, I hope there are no more*, he thought.

The lieutenant colonel then switched his phone on: there were messages telling him to ring headquarters. When he heard the news, Porter's response was the same as that of many other soldiers: 'No, not Bairdy. Not fucking Bairdy.'

The news wasn't any sadder than if any other commando had died, but it felt more surprising. Even though Tom Porter's last interactions with Cam had been to tell him to keep his head down, the idea that the Taliban had been able to kill him seemed unfathomable. Bairdy was a force of nature, but now he would be forever still.

Whenever a member of the armed forces dies, a notification officer is sent to inform the next of kin. In Cam's case, this was Doug and Kaye. The notification officer is usually followed by a padre; the officer remains with the loved ones only briefly, as the family permanently links the person telling the awful news with the news itself. The padre stays longer; representatives of the man's regiment also arrive, and 'wrap the arms of the unit around the family', as Porter puts it.

But Tom Porter was only a short trip from Doug and Kaye's home on the Gold Coast, so he felt honour-bound to be with them as soon as possible. He arranged to be on the next plane.

'Doug and Kaye were remarkable,' Porter recalls. 'It was likely the worst day of their lives, and the way they responded, humble and present, gave me a better understanding of why Cam was the way that he was.'

A new life started for Doug and Kaye Baird that day. The grief of losing a child is permanent and scarring, and can also be debilitating and disorientating. But amid the darkness of Cam's death, Doug and Kaye have chosen to push on in a deliberate direction. They're now the public custodians of the memory of their son, and speak regularly at functions in the service of raising money or awareness for charities that support veterans. Brendan joins them sometimes, but not often. I think he still finds speaking about Cam in public quite difficult.

After Cameron's death, when the grief had become less constant, Doug and Kaye Baird stepped up at every occasion they could to honour their son. In return, they would hear stories from his friends about the man he was. Often they learned things they'd never known.

'Most of our conversations were very short, but there were certain things he couldn't say and certain things he wouldn't say,' Doug says. 'All the events we attend now, there seems to be someone there who knew Cam, served with him, or a friend who has a story, a joke or a photo that has helped us to pull together a piece of his life.'

One emotional meeting Doug and Kaye had was with a young high-school student, Campbell Byrd, who, as part of a Year Seven class project, had written a letter to an unknown soldier in Afghanistan in May 2013. A month after the teacher had sent off the letters, Campbell received a reply from a Corporal Cameron Baird. Cam wrote the letter two weeks before he died. Recently, Kaye and Doug made its contents public, and revealed how it helped them better understand their son's work.

In that last letter, Cam wrote:

Sometimes my job is difficult but I have good reasons to do it. Making the world a safer place for others is one reason. I think we are very lucky in Australia, we are safe and can live our lives as we wish. Being away from family and friends is difficult but I have been in the Army for over 13 years and have become accustomed to being away.

Cameron signed off by saying: 'Always try your best in whatever you do, and always be happy in your life.'

Brendan Baird spoke powerfully at Cam's funeral, telling the story of how, as a young boy, he hit Cam in the head with a block of wood; even though blood was pouring from his face, Cam pretended to his parents that nothing had happened, because he only ever wanted good things for Brendan. Afterwards, a piper played 'Highway to Hell'. As Brendan sat down, he wore a face of pure devastation. I suspect the dual wounds Brendan has suffered – of his brother's killing and his wife's death – will never fully heal.

After Cam's death there had been a private communications ban in Tarin Kowt, to ensure that those closest to Cam didn't hear about his passing on the news or social media. In that period, Brendan took on the responsibility of telling the extended family and non-military friends what had happened to his brother.

Brendan spoke to Robin. I have not asked Robin about her response, but I imagine it would have been devastation. She truly loved Cam, and asked if she could attend the funeral. Kaye says she did see Robin at the back, in the crowd. 'I always felt she should have been up the front, with us,' she says.

After the public announcement of Cameron Baird's death, the Department of Defence distributed to the press a short statement and biography. The *Sydney Morning Herald* gave a bloodless account of the battle: 'Corporal

Baird had been killed during a special operations task group operation to disrupt an insurgent network in the Khod Valley.' There were also unimpeachable but impersonal statements by the Prime Minister and Opposition Leader, as well as the Defence Minister.

Cameron Baird's body was laid to rest in a cemetery on the Gold Coast, close to where Doug, Kaye and Brendan live. Cricket was front and centre at the funeral, and she too was shattered. As Cam's partner, she went through an exhausting sequence of public and private memorials; by the end, she just wanted to escape. The death of her boyfriend had seemingly become public property, and eventually all the public engagements, she felt, related more to Anzac myth than to the big, burly, funny, idiosyncratic bloke whom she loved. Cricket now lives in Singapore.

In 2014 Cam's schoolfriends banded together with Andrew Harrison, his teacher and first footy coach, to create Cam's Cause, a charity that benefits veterans' services, and especially the Commando Welfare Trust.

—

A little more than six months after Cam's death, the boys of Bravo Company were told to assemble at the base in Holsworthy. There, they crowded around a television showing ABC News 24. Presenter Joe O'Brien announced an interruption of regular programming: Prime Minister Tony Abbott was about to make a special announcement in parliament.

'I stand to solemnly inform the House, in the presence of family and defence chiefs, that the 100th Victoria Cross has been awarded to an Australian. Corporal Cameron Baird . . .'

At the mention of their mate, the gunfighters, officers and support staff of Bravo all erupted.

The Victoria Cross is the most hallowed of Australian military tributes. It's an honour that has been bestowed only four times since 1969, and eight times since the end of World War II. Posthumously, Cameron Baird has also had a number of other honours conferred upon him – memorial stamps and statues, even the naming of a staging base in the United Arab Emirates (which Cam always thought was full of pencil-pushers) – but there is no recognition he would be more proud of than the Victoria Cross. This is not because it's the highest individual honour an Australian soldier can win, but because it also honours his unit. Cam's Victoria Cross recognises the tempo, extremity and complexity of the fighting that his mates undertook in Afghanistan.

For Cameron Baird, being a soldier – a commando – came above all else.

CHAPTER NINETEEN

A LEGACY

'No man is an island, entire of itself; every man is a piece of the continent . . .'
'MEDITATION XVII', JOHN DONNE

Cam and the other commando gunfighters had a positive effect on Uruzgan and Afghanistan. In the time they were operating there, school attendance rates went up, child mortality rates went down and there was less general violence and lawlessness. The question of how that work relates to Australian interests, however, is more complicated.

When the SOTG rotations in Afghanistan began, Australia's stated goals were to destroy foreign terrorist networks and safe harbours, support and build the Afghan government and armed forces, and fulfil the Americans' expectations that Australia would support them in what was largely a US initiative. But by the time the SOTG arrived, the al-Qaeda network was already scattered, many of the powerful coalition Afghan partners were never going to support a centralised government, and simple participation is a strange reason to be in war. In retrospect, Australian forces essentially became actors in a largely intractable foreign civil war.

Many of the soldiers and officers of Bravo Company wonder whether there was ever an overall plan in Afghanistan. Each SOTG rotation started with short-term goals – destroying certain insurgent networks, attacking drug production areas, or supporting ISAF initiatives – but they now question whether those goals ever related to a broader strategy aimed at victory.

'I'd like to think that there's a document in a desk drawer somewhere in Canberra that explains how we planned to win the war, but I doubt it exists,' one officer told me.

If you travel to Uruzgan now (and doing so means taking your life in your hands) you'll find few reminders of Australia's involvement in the war. Tarin Kowt has an absurdly impressive airport, kids still sometimes carry round colouring books donated by Australian soldiers, and there are a lot of insurgent graves. But that's about it.

Matiullah Khan is dead, assassinated by the Taliban, and his scion Midow Khan has also been killed. The Khod

Valley is a Taliban stronghold. There's been a drastic increase in drug production, and the United Nations recently reported that thousands of internally displaced people are moving away from Tarin Kowt, fearful of governmental collapse and a Taliban takeover.

This is not to say, though, that the fighting in Afghanistan was all for nothing. Canberra and Washington may have failed strategically in Afghanistan, but on the battlefields of Uruzgan and Helmand the commandos learned to dominate, adapting and overcoming in a historically difficult battlespace. This is Cameron Baird's legacy. Sown in Afghanistan, it is now reaped at Holsworthy.

'If Australia had its baptism of fire in Gallipoli,' says Lieutenant Colonel Tom Porter, 'then the baptism of fire for the commando unit was Afghanistan – not defined by one battle, but by one campaign. As a very senior officer said to me once, the [2 Commando] unit was never supposed to get this good. When Afghanistan started we were very much the red-headed stepchild, but the people in the unit were in a position to decide what they were going to be.'

After Cam was killed, Bravo undertook one more mission as part of the SOTG. It wasn't particularly memorable, except for two things: all the gunfighters arrived at the choppers wearing the distinctive facial camouflage that Bairdy preferred, and the mission was in the exact area

313

where Rot Five's nursery patrol had been attacked. This mission was drastically different from that first nervous foray into that area by Cam and Bravo Company. This time they inserted by helicopter, and were ascendant in every gunfight.

—

2 Commando's evolution over just a few years was striking, and even more so when you consider what it was when Cameron Baird joined.

Back in 2000, when Cam arrived at the cell-like Tobruk Lines, 4RAR had aspirations that few thought it could fulfil so quickly. The unit had raised two commando companies then, and its other soldiers were regular infantrymen, fulfilling that role in East Timor and the Solomon Islands. The Army had announced that it was trying to raise a second special forces counter-terrorism force in the east, but the SASR men in the west, who understood what it meant to raise a 'black role', privately questioned whether the unit was capable of this – and whether it would ever be capable. When 4RAR was deployed to Iraq, the upper echelons of the Army had such little faith in the unit that they kept its men out of harm's way.

Then the Afghan rotations started. Initially, the SASR was always the force element of choice for complex and dangerous missions. Perth therefore got the best assets, the best intelligence and the best foreign partners. The commandos used relatively old equipment and conducted only vehicle and foot missions. The derogatory nickname 'tuna' bounced around, suggesting that 4RAR/2 Commando was for those soldiers whom (John) West rejected.

But the best soldiers in 2 Commando, men like Cam Baird, never bought into these tensions with the SASR. Instead, like ambitious immigrants, they attacked every dirty job, every small opportunity, and all with a singular, hungry focus. Any opportunity was a good opportunity.

With every Afghan rotation – every year, every mission, every gunfight – the commandos continued to evolve.

Those early rotations could have been disastrous for the commandos. Few of the soldiers, from Digger to commander, had any downrange experience. In instances like the one in Chenartu, when Cam found himself outside a doorway with metal spitting towards him, a friend shot dead and his team pinned down, mass-casualty events beckoned. If there had been a catastrophic moment for the young special forces unit, it's easy to imagine its short leash being yanked even harder, perhaps dragging the commandos all the way back to Sydney.

Through death, through exhaustion and sometimes through disrespect, Cam Baird and Bravo Company never lost their drive or desire. Setbacks and tragedies only spurred them on to work harder. By the end of the Afghan campaign, there was almost no difference between the work done by the east and west special forces gunfighting units.

'I don't think there're many differences between SAS and commandos now,' says Lieutenant Colonel Tom Porter. 'But the SAS values the individual, and that's often where their dominance is. Commandos are all about team before self, and that's where their power is.'

In no small part, this is due to the efficiency and dominance of the team commanders who operated in Afghanistan.

'If you are an organisation dedicated to warfighting, there's a lot of alpha males, and even in that context [Cameron Baird] stands out,' Porter says. 'People naturally file in behind people who are stronger than you, but in a unit like this with a lot of headstrong blokes, it means a lot to have people naturally lead you. I think [the team commanders] were the guys who would define the unit. They're junior enough that they can say and do what they want, but senior enough to command respect and authority. Cam was a major part of that.'

On the battlefield, every man in a commando company is necessarily expendable, but as soon as Cam was killed, his legacy was felt, with his men continuing the fight viciously but judiciously. His style of leadership, his reason, his work ethic and, most of all, his capacity for front-foot aggression bled into his team, and into his platoon and his company. With soldiers like Jeremy Thorne destined for team command, and possibly also duty at the Special Forces Training Centre at Holsworthy, this spirit will be in the DNA of the unit for decades to come.

The years of Cameron Baird's life were too few, but they were full and incredible. As a footballer, partner, son, brother, mate and soldier, he was as loyal and dedicated as he was indefatigable. In Afghanistan, Cameron Baird killed and was killed, with neither doubt nor fear in his heart. This is what it means to be an Aussie commando – because men like Cameron Baird decided that's what it should be.

Lest we forget.

GLOSSARY

1RAR: 1st Battalion, Royal Australian Regiment

2IC: second in command

4RAR: 4th Battalion, Royal Australian Regiment; later
4RAR, then 2 Commando

ADF: Australian Defence Force

AO: area of operations

ASLAV: Australian Light Armoured Vehicles

BSG: Baghdad Security Group

CASEVAC: casualty evacuation

CENTCOM: United States Central Command

CPA: Coalitional Provisional Authority

CQB: close-quarters battle

CSAR: combat search and rescue

CSM: company sergeant major

DEA: Drug Enforcement Administration

EA: Emergency Action commander

ECM: electronic counter-measures

FAST: Foreign-deployed Advisory and Support Team

FE: force element

FOB: Forward Operating Base

Fretilin: Revolutionary Front for an Independent
East Timor

FUP: forming-up point

HVT: high-value target

IED: improvised explosive device

INTERFET: International Force for East Timor

IO: investigating officer

IRR: Incident Response Regiment

ISAF: International Security Assistance Force

ISIS: Islamic State of Iraq and Syria

JDAM: Joint Direct Action Munitions

JPEL: Joint Prioritized Effects List

JSOC: Joint Special Operations Command

KIA: killed in action

LRPV: Long Range Patrol Vehicle

MEAO: Middle East Area of Operations

MNF: Multi-National Force

MRE: Meals Ready to Eat

NIU: Nation Interdiction Unit

NVGs: night-vision goggles

PRC: Provincial Response Company

PRT: Provincial Reconstruction Team

PTSD: post-traumatic stress disorder

QRF: quick reaction force

RPG: rocket-propelled grenade

RSM: Regimental Sergeant Major

SASR: Special Air Service Regiment

SOCOM: US Army Special Operations Command

SOER: Special Operations Engineer Regiment

SOTG: Special Operations Task Group

TAG: Tactical Assault Group

TFL: Tasmanian Football League

TK: Tarin Kowt, Afghanistan

TTP: techniques, tactics and procedure

UAV: unmanned aerial vehicle

USAID: United States Agency for International Development

VDO: vehicle drop-off

VMMD: Vehicle Mounted Mine Detector

WMD: weapons of mass destruction

TRIBUTES TO CORPORAL CAMERON BAIRD VC, MG

After Cameron's death his parents, Kaye and Doug Baird, received many tributes to their son. Some were from the upper echelons of Australia's defence force, some were from his fellow soldiers, some were from people who had known Cameron as a young man and some from those he had connected with fleetingly. Kaye and Doug would like to share just a few of these tributes.

> *This man was a decorated soldier. In combat and as a team commander, he was the man to watch and was never happier than when the situation demanded decisive action and courage. He was described by colleagues as one of the most iconic figures in the regiment. Corporal Baird was a modern-day warrior who set a standard that every soldier aspires to achieve.*
>
> – General David Hurley, Chief of Defence

Corporal Baird was a courageous soldier, a first-rate leader.

– Chief of Army Lieutenant General David Morrison

Corporal Baird never took a backward step, he was an experienced, combat-hardened soldier who always led from the front, getting the best out of those who worked alongside him.

– Special Operations Commander Major General
Peter 'Gus' Gilmore

We mourn the loss of a great soldier, one who led from the front and whose was a life of stunning accomplishments, he will never be forgotten by his regiment, his Army or his nation.

– Lieutenant Colonel B, Commanding Officer,
2 Commando Regiment

Cameron Baird is and will always be one of the most inspiring leaders within 2 Commando Regiment. There is not one of us who would not follow him into any combat situation. His moral, physical and mental standards provided a guiding light for each of us to follow. He will never be forgotten.

– Major P, Cameron's commanding officer

Corporal Baird's actions epitomised the courage and quick thinking needed to be a Commando. He was just a dynamo in that unit. Even though his weapon failed, he fixed the weapon and got straight back into the battle. And it's that kind of momentum that needs to be continued to win the firefight. I believe Cameron Baird was one of Australia's greatest ever soldiers.

– Warrant Officer Dave Ashley
(Army Regimental Sergeant Major)

Cameron was a favourite son at Gladstone Park High and all the teachers and fellow students who came into contact with him held him in the highest regard . . . I was so impressed with his humility and empathy for others. He knew his ability and never for a moment displayed anything but a selfless attitude.

– Len Hannah, former teacher at
Gladstone Park Secondary College

CORPORAL CAMERON BAIRD – HONOURS AND AWARDS

- Victoria Cross for Australia

- Medal for Gallantry

- Australian Active Service Medal with 'East Timor', 'Iraq 2003' and International Coalition Against Terrorism (ICAT) clasps

- Afghanistan Medal

- Iraq Medal

- Australian Service Medal with 'Counter Terrorism / Special Recovery (CT/SR)' clasps

- Australian Defence Medal

- United Nations Medal with Ribbon United Nations Transitional Authority in East Timor

- NATO Meritorious Service Medal

- NATO Non-Article 5 Medal with 'International Security Assistance Force (ISAF)' and multi-tour indicator '3'

- Meritorious Unit Citation – Task Force 66 (Special Operations Task Group), Afghanistan

- Infantry Combat Badge

- Returned from Active Service Badge

FIVE YEARS ON

KAYE AND DOUG BAIRD

Five years on from Cameron's death, we have been surprised (and pleased) that the interest in Cameron's story is stronger than ever. We are proud that our son is now seen by so many as a representative of the modern-day ANZAC and that he is held in such high esteem by his fellow soldiers. For Cameron, that would be the greatest accolade, to be respected by his mates. Cameron's dedication to duty and to his country, the values he held close and the way he kept faith with those values in his life and on the battlefield were outlined admirably in this book by Ben Mckelvey. The responses from readers have been heartwarming for us. There have been television programs, documentaries and a featured display at the Australian War Memorial about Cameron, and so many print media stories that we have almost lost count. There has also been feature film interest. Having the general public learn more about Cameron and the way his name is aligned with the words resilience, dedication, focus, duty, bravery and mateship is very important to us.

Cameron's job as a soldier and a Special Forces Commando saw him trained to fight to protect our great country and his fellow soldiers. The reality of life for a combat soldier is that in fighting and engaging with the enemy, injury or death are always possible. Cameron knew this well and before his death he had witnessed good friends die in battle. He knew what war can do and what had to be done. He fought with controlled aggression and understood the intent of his commanding officers. He knew the objectives and every day he set out to make sure they were achieved. Our son retained his sense of humanity as much as is possible while engaged in deadly combat. His sense of empathy and understanding may have been tested, but they held firm, and in the last years of his life he was always reading and searching to connect with other people, and learning about other ways to live an honourable life.

These past five years have been very hard for us. The loss of Cameron does not ever diminish and we carry that grief every day. But to have been supported by Army and encouraged to act as Cameron's representative at significant historical events in Australia and overseas has helped us keep his name and legacy alive. We will continue to honour his Victoria Cross and Medal of Gallantry awards and keep his name forever linked to these. Like too many other parents who lost their children in the Afghanistan campaign (or any other military engagement), we may never find peace with Cameron's death, but we try to create some good from this sadness. To this end, the charity set up in his name, Cam's Cause, has already raised more than $100,000 to support 2nd Commando Regiment and the Commando Welfare Trust.

Cameron's regiment, the 2nd Commando, is our country's highest decorated regiment over the last ten years and their soldiers regularly lead from the front in battle. They are known for their focus, dedication and discipline and because they do a great deal of the heavy lifting they have paid a very big price for our country, with the most KIA or wounded recorded. To be able to support them is something we know Cameron would be pleased about. To provide support and funds for soldiers with PTSD and physical and mental injuries is vital to us. We have seen the suffering of Cameron's fellow soldiers who came home still battling their own war. We have been to one too many funerals for good men and with Cam's Cause we will do all we can to provide assistance to them and prevent PTSD claiming more lives.

Cameron has been honoured in many big and small ways since his death.

The Tasmanian government has implemented a $2500 scholarship that will be awarded each year to anyone who has displayed outstanding community involvement and is joining the Australian Defence Force; the City of Hume has a $5000 scholarship for the most outstanding youth involved in their community; several schools in Victoria and Tasmania have plaques in their school gardens dedicated to Cameron and a number of schools have added 'Cameron' as a name for one of their school houses; and rooms in Burnie RSL and in Albury/Wodonga have been named after him. Four medals have been struck in Cameron's name in various grades of AFL – the captain of the Victorian Primary School team receives the Corporal Cameron Baird VC, MG Medal and the Australian Army Tri-services Series best male and female players, Redland Sharks Best Player in the Anzac round, Burnie Dockers and the Calder Cannons all award medals or trophies after Cameron for either best on ground or most courageous player. During basic training at Kapooka, the soldier chosen as most outstanding in the platoon is awarded the Cpl Cameron Baird VC, MG Award. We are very proud and appreciative of this recognition.

It was said by one of Cameron's commanding officers that in death Cam will probably grow a few inches as his story is told and he changes from unit icon in life to an Australian legend in death. We don't want Cameron to be seen as anything other than the man he was. We all have flaws and Cameron was no different. But as a soldier he brought the best of himself to his duty and as a man the characteristics of strength of spirit, focus, determination, bravery, resilience and upholding mateship that he displayed so often are what we hope will always be linked to the name Cameron Baird.

We hope that we will be working with Army headquarters and their Chief of Staff Office for many years to come to represent Cameron. In telling his story we are able to tell the history of Australia's recent military conflicts and what it means to be a serving soldier, fighting for our country. Through him, the importance of the ANZAC spirit can be shown. We also hope that his name will continue to help drive the charity work focused on helping veterans. If Cameron's legacy enables returned soldiers and their families to find some comfort and relief, then his death will be just that little bit easier to bear.

Kaye and Doug Baird
May 2018

2 COMMANDO HONOUR ROLL

*'They shall not grow old, as we that are left grow
old. Age shall not weary them, nor the years
condemn. At the going down of the sun and
in the morning, we will remember them.'*

Corporal Cameron Stewart Baird VC, MG

Private Nathanael John Aubrey Galagher

Lance Corporal Mervyn John McDonald

Sergeant Todd Matthew Langley

Sergeant Brett Matthew Wood, MG DSM

Private Scott Travis Palmer

Private Benjamin Adam Chuck

Private Timothy James Aplin

Lance Corporal Mason Kerrin Edwards

Lieutenant Michael Kenneth Housdan Fussell

Lance Corporal Jason Paul Marks

Private Luke James Worsley

*We also acknowledge the sacrifice and loss of all other
fallen soldiers and their families.*

'BURNIE BOY'

Just a Tassie boy from Burnie town
with a smile as big as the moon,
Made his mum and dad so proud
that day he came in June.
Born for purpose and a destined path
this little boy grew big.
With seasons that pushed him towards his fate,
young Cam became a dig.
With a humble heart and determined will,
success became his prey.
The commando in him exploded out,
a legend was born that day.
With spirit and honour Cam went to war,
over and over again,
his courage shone and inspired all,
was aggressive but so humane.
A fearless leader, he led from the front,
his enemy shuttered with fear.
He made the hairs on their neck stand up,
whenever he was near.
The enemy out front, his team behind,
Cam charged towards the foe.
Each step he took, was for his mates
and mercy he didn't show.
His family, his mates and all that mattered
were the last things on his mind,
as he fell to the Earth, and took his last breath,
and left it all behind.
This was the plan, God had all along,
to teach us how we should live.
Living your life as a sacrifice,
not to take but how you should give.
So rest in peace young Burnie boy,
Your legacy will remain.
For the debt you paid, we'll never forget,
for it fuels the eternal flame.

Corporal E Rowland, in loving memory of Corporal Cameron Baird VC, MG

ACKNOWLEDGMENTS

KAYE AND DOUG BAIRD:

We would like to thank many people for their support over the last few years, and for their help with this book.

To all in the Australian Army and Australian Defence Force, the soldiers of the 2nd Commando Regiment (Special Forces) and Cameron's fellow soldiers in 2 Commando Bravo Company, thank you.

To Governor-General Sir Peter Cosgrove and Lady Cosgrove and to the staff at Government House, thank you for your help and kindness.

To the Department of Veterans Affairs (DVA) and to Minister Dan Tehan, thank you. The Baird family also wishes to encourage the DVA to continue to look for better and faster ways to find solutions and process all veteran's claims!

Thank you also to Major General Dave Chalmers (Retired) and staff; Dr Brendan Nelson, the Australian War Memorial and all the staff there; and to all the people involved in the Cam's Cause charity – thank you.

To the management and staff of Currumbin RSL, we'd like to thank you for looking after us and for giving the statue of Cameron a wonderful home.

To our family and friends, your support has been invaluable. Thank you also to Nishara Miles and Captain Darren Elder, our Army family and VC Posthumous Management/Welfare Advisors – we don't know how we would have managed without you.

To all the staff at Hachette Australia, thank you for helping us put the book together.

And, finally, to Ben Mckelvey, you have done a wonderful job in telling Cameron's story.

BEN MCKELVEY:

This book could never have been possible without the efforts of Doug, Kaye and Brendan Baird. They were not only welcoming but wonderful as they helped me write this book, and their kindness while undertaking a difficult duty is something I'll never forget. The men of 2 Commando, and especially the gunfighters of Bravo Company, I also owe a very special debt to. They were available, truthful, thoughtful and incredible, and a special mention must go to Eddie Robertson, who I suspect vouched for me early in the process. I owe you a beer, mate. Thanks must also go to the people at Hachette Australia and especially my publisher Vanessa Radnidge; a lovely woman and one of the greatest assets an author or book subject could ever ask for.

INDEX

CAM'S CAUSE

Cam's Cause is a not-for-profit organisation founded in 2014 by friends and family of Corporal Cameron Baird VC, MG, who have forged a partnership to uphold Cameron's life motto of 'Aspire to Inspire'.

Cam's Cause achieved registered charity status in 2016 and is also a registered deductible gift recipient.

Cameron was an exceptionally modest man who, when on home soil, spent significant time supporting organisations that raised money for soldier welfare. Well over 259 soldiers have been permanently affected by physical injuries sustained in battle. What is more alarming are the increasing numbers of psychological injuries that soldiers are facing such as Post Traumatic Stress Disorder (PTSD), depression and anxiety.

Cam's Cause aims to raise much needed funds to help build specially designed camps that provide a unique environment incorporating general outdoor activities and specialist help that have been created by 2 Commando Regiment's Human Performance Wing. These camps have been created for Commandos by Commandos and are proven to make a difference in assisting recovery from physical and mental injuries.

www.camscause.org

BEN MCKELVEY is a bestselling author and journalist from Sydney. *The Commando* is his third book. His previous books are *Born to Fight* (with Mark Hunt) and *Songs of a War Boy* (with Deng Thiak Adut), which was shortlisted for the Victorian Premier's Literary Award and Australian Book Industry Award for biography.